Chocolate Lover's Guide™ COOKBOOK

The Best Chocolate Recipes
From Top Chefs and Bakers
In Oregon, Washington,
and British Columbia

BOBBIE HASSELBRING

The Chocolate Traveler

Wordsworth Publishing

Printed in the United States.

ISBN 0-9665619-1-0

Cover design: Marty Urman, MU Graphics
Interior design, layout, and illustration: Marty Urman, MU Graphics
Recipe formatting: Linda Faus, Home Economist
Proofreading: Neshama Franklin

Recipe Testers: Edward L. Alpen, Steve Beard, Lark Brandt, Celeste Cafiero, Rhonda Clark, Colin Cameron, Janene Clark, Kim Cook, Diana Vineyard Copeland, Tim Daly, Angela Dodson, Katherine Dunn, Jennifer Flanagan, Kathy Godare, Kathy Grinager, Mandy Groom, Bobbie Hasselbring, Randall Hatfield, Susan Hauser, Delores Kilpela, Kathy Leonard, Marilyn McFarlane, Donna Matrazzo, Nancy Medici, Charrise Nunnink, Ella Nuttbrock, Amy Pelsey, Annie Peterson, Andrea Rapp, Steve Smith, Susan Stanley, Anne Weaver, Kristin Wood.

Author photo: Anne Weaver Photography
Cover photo: Fleuri Restaurant's Chocoholic Bar, Vancouver, British Columbia © Sutton Place Hotel. Photo used with permission.

Wordsworth Publishing
P.O. Box 311
Beavercreek, OR 97004
(503) 632-4610
(877) 800-7700 (toll-free)
(503) 632-6754 (fax)
hasselbring@email.msn.com

Disclaimer: The recipes in this book were provided by various restaurants, bakeries, and inns in the Pacific Northwest. The author and the publisher have made every effort to ensure the recipes are accurate. In addition, all the recipes have been tested by home cooks or by professional chefs. However, errors may occur in a book of this nature. In addition, some of the recipes call for the use of raw eggs or other ingredients some individuals may be sensitive to. The author, the businesses and individuals featured, and Wordsworth Publishing assume no responsibility or liability for any loss or injury incurred by the use of these recipes.

Publisher's Cataloging-in-Publication
  (Provided by Quality Books, Inc.)

Hasselbring, Bobbie, 1951-
    The chocolate lover's guide cookbook / Bobbie
  Hasselbring -- 1st ed.
    p. cm.
    Includes index.
    ISBN: 0-9665619-1-0

    1. Cookery (Chocolate) 2. Chocolate.
  3. Cookery, American--Pacific Northwest style.
  I. Hasselbring, Bobbie, 1951- Chocolate lover's
  guide to the Pacific Northwest. II. Title.

TX767.C5H37 1999   641.6'374
                QBI99-859

This book is dedicated to

My mother, Marguerite Arlene Clarke,
who always kept a box of chocolates on her bedside table

and

Michael Castleman,
my friend and mentor for many years

The Chocolate Lover's Guide™ COOKBOOK

Acknowledgements

Many people contributed to *The Chocolate Lover's Guide Cookbook*. I'd like to thank Marty Urman of MU Graphics for her artistic expertise. Home economist and recipe expert extradinaire, Linda Faus, spent many hours deciphering and re-formatting the recipes. Without her, this book would not have happened

It is with great humility and gratitude that I thank the people who used their time, skills, and resources to test and re-test the recipes: Edward L. Alpen, Steve Beard, Lark Brandt, Celeste Cafiero, Rhonda Clark, Colin Cameron, Kim Cook, Diana Vineyard Copeland, Janene Clark, Tim Daly, Angela Dodson, Katherine Dunn, Jennifer Flanagan, Kathy Godare, Kathy Grinager, Mandy Groom, Randall Hatfield, Susan Hauser, Delores Kilpela, Kathy Leonard, Marilyn McFarlane, Donna Matrazzo, Nancy Medici, Charrise Nunnink, Ella Nuttbrock, Amy Pelsey, Annie Peterson, Andrea Rapp, Steve Smith, Susan Stanley, Anne Weaver, Kristin Wood. Your generosity is wonderful!

I'm grateful for the continued support of friends, family, and colleagues, including Heidi Yorkshire, Michael Castleman, and Anne Weaver. In addition, I'd like to thank my colleagues at Northwest Association of Book Publishers.

Most of all, I'd like to thank the chefs, bakers, chocolatiers, innkeepers, and restaurant owners who shared their delectable recipes and made *The Chocolate Lover's Guide Cookbook* a reality.

"O sweet liquor
sent from the stars,
Surely you must be
the drink of the gods!"

excerpt from "Ode to Chocolate" by Aloysius Ferronius, 1664

I can't remember a time I didn't love chocolate. Every birthday, my choice was chocolate cake with chocolate frosting. On Saturdays when Mrs. Periera would take us to J.J. Newberry's for ice cream, I'd order a double scoop of chocolate chip. And when the Helm's Bread truck drove through the neighborhood, I couldn't wait to bite into a crunchy-fresh chocolate cake doughnut with chocolate icing. As a grownup, my passion for chocolate hasn't dwindled. It's expanded. I still like chocolate cake, chocolate chip ice cream, and chocolate cake doughnuts. Now I also like chocolate truffles, chocolate ganache torte, chocolate soufflé, chocolate silk, chocolate cheesecake, chocolate crème brulee, chocolate mousse, chocolate semifreddo, chocolate paté, chocolate roulade, chocolate marjolaine, chocolate terrine, chocolate bombes, and more, so much more. As the adage goes, "there's so much chocolate and so little time."

If you're a chocolate lover like me, you understand why I spent a year of my life traveling and sampling chocolate to bring you *The Chocolate Lover's Guide*™ *to the Pacific Northwest* and now *The Chocolate Lover's Guide*™ *Cookbook*. I criss-crossed the Pacific Northwest, traveling nearly 12,000 miles and sampling more than 2,000 desserts from 700+ restaurants, bakeries, ice creameries, and chocolate shops. When a dessert was especially wonderful, I'd ask for the recipe. The restaurant owners, chefs, bakers, pastry chefs, and chocolatiers were incredibly generous in sharing their secrets. The result is *The Chocolate Lover's Guide Cookbook*, 102 recipes for cakes, tortes, soufflés, tarts, pies, brownies and cookies, ice cream, puddings, and specialty chocolate desserts, representing some of the very best chocolate being made today in Oregon, Washington, and British Columbia.

The Chocolate Lover's Guide Cookbook **will appeal to the beginning cook as well as to the advanced.** It contains recipes ranging from simple to quite complex. Recipes like Hello Dolly Bars or Chez Daniel's Classic Truffles are so simple and bulletproof that novice cooks can be successful with them. Other recipes like Chocolate Medallions and Chocolate-Raspberry Bombes are more time-consuming and will challenge sophisticated cooks.

You may wonder why we've chosen to include multiple versions of some recipes. It's because each recipe has its own unique personality. I was amazed, for instance, that chocolate mousse could have so many variations. Some recipes are velvety smooth and light as air. Others are denser with a deep chocolate flavor. Still others are chunky and chewy. All of them are excellent. We include different versions so that you can experiment and find the one(s) that are your personal favorites.

Unlike the recipes published in many cookbooks today, all of the recipes in *The Chocolate Lover's Guide Cookbook* have been thoroughly tested by home cooks and professional cooks. In many cases, the recipes are exactly as the original chefs wrote them, with only formatting changes to make them easier to follow. In other cases, the recipes have been adapted to make them more successful for the home cook. Some recipes have Chef's notes, comments or suggestions from the person who submitted the recipe. Others have Recipe Tester notes, remarks from those who tested the recipes.

The information in the Tips, Tools, Techniques, and Temperatures and Timing sections, as well as the Glossary and Appendices, will appeal to different types of cooks. For some of you, the information will be "old hat." Others may have "ah ha" reactions, saying, "Oh, that's how they do that!" or "I didn't know that." Whatever level cook you are, it's my hope that the information and recipes presented here will help you make beautiful and delicious chocolate desserts to delight you, your friends, and your family. Enjoy!

Bobbie Hasselbring
The Chocolate Traveler

Tips for Making
Terrific Chocolate Desserts

The quality of the ingredients you use in your recipes will determine the quality of your finished desserts. I tasted one of the recipes in this book after it had been made with an inferior-quality chocolate. The difference in the flavor and texture was so dramatic, I didn't recognize it as the same recipe! I adhere to the advice of veteran pastry chef Han Weiss, owner of Han's in Bend, Oregon, "Use only the best. If you use the best, you'll get the best out of your recipes."

Yes, many of these recipes are expensive to make. That's because they call for wonderfully delicious ingredients like high-quality chocolate, real butter, cream, fresh nuts, and mascarpone cheese. My attitude is that life is short and wonderful desserts help make life worthwhile. And besides, don't you deserve wonderfully decadent desserts? If you really can't justify the cost, just enjoy reading the recipes–perhaps while eating a box of good chocolates.

Butter - Many of the recipes call for sweet or unsalted butter. That's because chocolate doesn't need the added salt and the salt can overwhelm other subtle flavors in recipes. Also, salted butter contains moisture absorbed by the salt, which can alter the fat-liquid ratio in the recipes. The salt in butter does help preserve it. If you keep unsalted butter on hand, keep it in the freezer for freshness. Remove it from the freezer an hour or so before you need it for your recipe.

When a recipe calls for butter (sweet or salted), don't substitute margarine or shortening. Otherwise you probably won't get good results. If a recipe calls for margarine, use a margarine that contains at least 80% vegetable oil. Margarines with less than 80% vegetable oil (vegetable oil spreads, reduced, diet, lite, liquid, soft, or whipped margarine) have lots of water in them. They are not intended for baking and will not yield good results.

Chocolate -"What's the Best Chocolate?" I asked hundreds of chefs, pastry chefs, chocolatiers, and bakers. I received dozens of answers--Callebaut, Blommer, Guittard, Nestlé, Ghiradelli, Valhrona, Scharffen Berger, Merckens, and El Rey, among others. Some prefer smooth, creamy chocolate like Belgian. Others like sharper tastes like those found in Valhrona, El Rey or Scharffen Berger chocolate. Everyone insisted their chocolate choice was best. I was left still wondering, "What is the best chocolate?"

The best answer came from long-time chocolatier Iva Elmer, who, with her husband, Jack, co-owns JaCiva's Chocolates and Pastries in Portland, Oregon. "What's the best chocolate? It's not bittersweet or milk chocolate. It's the chocolate you like. I know a woman who loves the chocolate in Almond Joy. For her, that's the best chocolate. It's what you like. That's the best chocolate for you."

All great chocolates–no matter the brand or manufacturer–share certain qualities. The old adage, "you get what you pay for," generally applies when it comes to chocolate. Some higher-quality chocolate is more expensive because it contains more expensive varieties of cacao beans. It's also conched or blended longer, making it smoother. Conching breaks down the chocolate solids into tiny pieces and coats the chocolate solids with cocoa butter. The result is chocolate that feels silky smooth on the tongue with no gritty or grainy quality.

Higher-quality chocolates also have a higher cocoa butter content. Cocoa butter is an expensive ingredient and one that is replaced in less expensive chocolate with other ingredients like vegetable shortening, and additional sugar, paraffin, and vanilla. Good quality chocolate with its high cocoa butter content not only feels silky, it begins to melt as soon as it hits the tongue. Quality chocolate never has a waxy or oily quality.

Look for These Qualities in Chocolate
- ✔ Velvety smoothness- never gritty or grainy
- ✔ Quick melt
- ✔ Intense flavor
- ✔ Shiny look
- ✔ Clean snap when broken

Always use real chocolate. Pure chocolate will contain chocolate liquor (no alcohol), sugar, cocoa butter, and perhaps lecithin and vanilla or vanillin. Milk chocolate will have these ingredients plus powdered milk. Imitation chocolate, which is sometimes mislabeled as chocolate, contains vegetable oil instead of cocoa butter. We don't recommend using imitation chocolate. Read labels to ensure you're getting real chocolate.

Buy the best chocolate you can afford. It will make a difference. All of the recipes included here were made with the highest quality chocolates.

Types of Chocolate. Many of the recipes specify the type of chocolate to be used. It's a good idea to follow the recommendations, especially since each type and brand has different cocoa butter and sugar contents, which can affect the recipe outcome. Whenever cocoa is called for, it's unsweetened cocoa.

- **Unsweetened Chocolate** - Also called bitter or baking chocolate, unsweetened chocolate is pure chocolate liquor with no sugar added. It consists of cocoa powder and cocoa butter. By law, it must contain a minimum of 50% and a maximum of 58% cocoa butter. It has an intense flavor. It's used primarily for baking recipes to which sugar or other sweeteners are added.

• **Semi-sweet or Bittersweet Chocolate -** This is chocolate liquor to which sweeteners and cocoa butter have been added. It's the darkest eating chocolate. It contains at least 35% chocolate liquor and has added cocoa butter to make it melt easily. Fat content averages 27%. Semi- or bittersweet chocolate is often used for making chocolate chips, garnishes, and making and coating baked goods.

• **Sweet or Dark Chocolate -** This chocolate contains more sweeteners than semi-sweet or bittersweet chocolate. It's used in making chocolate chips, candy bars, candy coating, and bakery items like cookies. Sweet chocolate contains 15-35% chocolate liquor and has about the same fat content as semi-sweet. The types and percentages of different cacao beans determine the flavor. It's used primarily for decorating and garnishing.

• **Milk Chocolate -** This is the most common form of eating chocolate in the United States. Milk chocolate is made by adding cocoa butter, milk, sweeteners, and flavorings to chocolate liquor. It contains at least 10% chocolate liquor and 12% milk solids. The flavor is typically a soft chocolate with milky or caramelized undertones. Milk chocolate is often used for making chocolate chips and candy bars.

• **White Chocolate -** Although it contains cocoa butter, white chocolate does not have any chocolate liquor in it so it's not considered real chocolate. In 1984, the U.S. Food and Drug Administration advised manufacturers not to use the term "white chocolate," but it's still used. White chocolate contains sugar, cocoa butter, milk solids and flavorings, usually vanilla. It's often used to make white chocolate chips and candy bars, and to coat baked goods.

• **Unsweetened Cocoa -** The least fatty form of chocolate, cocoa is chocolate with the cocoa butter removed. It's often used in baked goods or to make syrups or ice cream. Cocoas labeled "Dutch Process" or "European-style" have been treated with an alkalizing agent to neutralize naturally-occurring acids. The result is a mellower flavored cocoa with a reddish color.

• **Chocolate Flavored Coating -** Although not really chocolate, we include chocolate flavored coating here because there's so much confusion about it. Chocolate flavored coating consists of a blend of cocoa powder and vegetable fat (not cocoa butter). It often also contains sugar, milk, and flavorings. Because vegetable fat is less expensive than cocoa butter, chocolate flavored coating (dark or white) is cheaper than real chocolate. Some cooks opt for chocolate flavored coating because it does not have to be tempered like chocolate before using as a coating. However, these coatings often have a waxy mouthfeel and don't have the rich flavor of real chocolate. We don't recommend them.

• **Pre-melted Chocolate -** Packets of this semi-liquid, unsweetened cocoa powder and vegetable oil can be found on supermarket shelves in the baking section. These products are used exclusively for baking. While they are easy to use, we recommend using real melted chocolate.

• **Dietetic Chocolate -** This is sweet, bittersweet, or milk chocolate made with a sugar substitute like sorbitol or mannitol. Dietetic chocolate is made for those on sugar-restricted, not calorie-restricted, diets as dietetic chocolate may contain more calories than regular chocolate.

Substitutions

1 ounce unsweetened baking chocolate =
3 tablespoons cocoa + 1 tablespoon butter

6 ounces semi-sweet chocolate chips =
2 ounces unsweetened chocolate + 7 tablespoons sugar
+ 2 tablespoons shortening

14 ounce bar sweet baking chocolate =
3 tablespoons cocoa + 4 1/2 tablespoons granulated sugar
+ 2 2/3 tablespoons shortening

White chocolate cannot be directly substituted for dark chocolate because of the differing proportions of sugar and fat. However, it can be used for any recipe for the outside coating instead of dark chocolate. It must be tempered the same way as dark chocolate.

Chocolate Crumbs - Several of the recipes call for chocolate crumbs. This caused confusion for some of our recipe testers. "Are we supposed to scrape out the filling of Oreos?" one novice cook asked. We laughed and then realized other cooks might not know where to get chocolate crumbs. We recommend Nabisco Famous Chocolate Wafers™ for making chocolate crumbs. They're rich tasting and thin, which makes them easy to crumble. They're available in most supermarkets, but often not in the cookie/cracker section. In this author's local market, Nabisco Famous Chocolate Wafers™ are on a shelf next to the ice cream and ice cream cones. If you can't find them, ask your grocer. (In some Canadian markets, we've seen boxes of Oreo cookie crumbs, which are also excellent. However, we haven't seen them in U.S. markets.)

To make chocolate crumbs, place several chocolate wafers in a heavy-duty, zipper-style plastic bag. Push out the excess air before sealing. Then crush the wafers with a rolling pin.

Crème Fraiche - This is a matured, thickened cream with a tangy flavor and velvety texture. It's like a mild version of sour cream. You can substitute an equal amount of sour cream for crème fraiche. However, your recipe will have a slightly sharper flavor. You can easily make your own crème fraiche.

Crème Fraiche
1/2 cup whipping cream (not ultra-pasteurized cream)
1 teaspoon buttermilk (or yogurt or sour cream)

Start the crème fraiche at least two days before using it.

Stir the buttermilk into the whipping cream. Place in a warm place and allow to stand until it thickens to the consistency of yogurt or sour cream (8-24 hours). Refrigerate. Can be refrigerated for up to 10 days. It can be spooned over fresh fruit, warm cobblers, or used in sauces or soups (it can be boiled without curdling).

Dried Sour Cherries - Some of the recipes call for dried sour cherries, which can be difficult to find and rather expensive. Specialty food stores often carry them. They're less expensive at discount specialty stores like Trader Joe's. We recommend Montmorency Dried Sour Cherries™.

Eggs - Unless otherwise specified, all the recipes call for large eggs. Always use fresh, uncracked eggs. Use eggs well before the date stamped on the carton. To test the freshness of an egg, submerge it in a bowl of water. If it floats to the top, discard it.

Raw Egg Caution: Some recipes contain raw egg. There is a small risk of salmonella contamination in raw eggs. If you choose to make a recipe with raw eggs, use only fresh, uncracked eggs and refrigerate the dish promptly after making. Do not serve dishes made with raw eggs to anyone with a compromised immune system (women who are pregnant, people with chronic illnesses, the elderly or very young children).

Flavoring Extracts and Oils - Often, the flavors of flavoring extracts are disappointing and overwhelmed by the alcohol used in them. If a recipe calls for flavoring, opt for flavoring oils instead. They are usually available at specialty food stores or through mail order.

Ganache - Ganache is a combination of sweet cream and fine-quality chocolate. This rich chocolate-cream combination is used in making truffles, chocolate sauce, ice creams, and to cover or coat baked items. Ganache should be made with scalded, not boiled, cream (bubbles should appear on the sides of the saucepan). Most ganaches will set up in the refrigerator in about 4 hours. The shallower the container, the faster the ganache will set. You can make ganache a day or even a week or more ahead.

Liqueurs and Liquors - Almost any liqueur or liquor marries well with chocolate. However, sometimes it takes a day or so for the flavors to develop. For instance, if you taste ganache immediately after adding a liqueur flavor, the flavor may not seem strong enough. Don't add more. The flavors will develop as the ganache cools. We don't recommend adding more liqueur or liquor than the recipes specify.

Nuts - Nuts and chocolate make an excellent combination and many of the recipes in this book call for almonds, hazelnuts, walnuts, etc. Always use fresh nuts. Smell the nuts before buying, especially in the summer months when improper storage and heat can turn the nut oils rancid. If the nuts smell like insecticide, moldy, or musty, go to another store.

You can store nuts in the freezer in plastic freezer bags. Otherwise, they can turn rancid and ruin the flavor of your dessert. Nuts that have been exposed to high humidity will absorb moisture and will turn to mush when you grind them. If recipes require ground nuts, grind them before freezing.

Praline - A confection made of ground almonds or hazelnuts and sugar for chocolates, praline was named for the French Duke of Plessis-Praslin in 1671. Europeans use the term "praline" for individual pieces of a variety of fine chocolates.

Some specialty stores and mail order suppliers (see Resources) carry praline or praline powder. If you can't locate it, you can easily make your own.

Nut Praline
1 cup roasted, skinned hazelnuts, almonds, or pecans
1/2 cup granulated sugar
2 tablespoons water.

Butter a cookie sheet.

In a small, heavy saucepan or skillet, heat sugar and water. Swirl gently from time to time until the sugar and water come to a boil. Reduce heat to medium-high, cover pan, and continue boiling for 2 minutes. Uncover pan and boil for another 2 minutes, without stirring, until sugar turns a deep golden color. Watch carefully as sugar syrup burns quickly. Immediately remove from heat and stir in nuts. Turn the mixture onto the buttered cookie sheet and spread as thinly as possible. Cool until hardened.

For chunky praline, place cooled praline in a heavy plastic bag and pound bag with heavy spoon, mallet, or rolling pin. For praline powder, keep pounding until the praline becomes a powder. Or place cooled praline into the bowl of a food processor and grind into a powder.

Sourdough - A yeasty starter for leavening bread, muffins, and hot cakes, sourdough starter can add an interesting tang to chocolate recipes. Sourdough starter is available at specialty food markets, by mail order, or you can make your own. Keep in mind that sourdough starter must be "fed" regularly and, if it is left untended for too long, it can spoil.

Sourdough Starter
2 cups flour
1 package dry yeast or 1 yeast cake
2 cups warm water

Use only glass or pottery containers (no metal pans or utensils). Mix ingredients together. Place in a warm place or cupboard overnight. In the morning, put 1/2 cup of the starter in a pint jar (scald the jar first), cover with a tight lid, and place in the refrigerator or cool place. Use the remaining batter for pancakes, waffles, etc.

Every few days, add a little flour and water. This will keep the starter fresh and alive. Use as needed in recipes.

Sugar - The sugar specified in these recipes is common white granulated sugar. Powered or confectioners' sugar usually has 3% cornstarch added to prevent caking and should not be used in place of granulated sugar, especially in cooked sugar recipes.

Vanilla - Real vanilla extract is readily available at grocery stores. Although it's more expensive than imitation vanilla, we highly recommend the real thing. You may be able to find real vanilla at better prices at warehouse stores or specialty discount markets.

Take a moment and read through the entire recipe before starting. There's nothing more frustrating than getting half way through a recipe and discovering the recipe takes two days to prepare (and you have guests coming in a few hours). Or that you don't have the right ingredients or tools to complete it. Some of the recipes require time for baking, cooling, or resting dough, sometimes overnight. In addition, some of the recipes require ingredients and/or specialized tools you may not have on hand. Save yourself the aggravation and read through the entire recipe first.

Tools

Working with chocolate requires few specialized tools. However, the tools listed here will make your job easier and your recipes more successful.

Baker's piping or pastry bag. A baker's piping bag is a wonderful tool for making beautiful decorations with melted chocolate or buttercream, or for filling pastry cups with soft fillings like chocolate mousse. Coated fabric or plastic piping bags with decorating tips can be found at specialty food stores or baking supply companies (see Appendix I). Or you can make your own throw-away piping bag.

> 1. Cut a parchment paper rectangle (8 x 10 inches). Then cut the paper in half diagonally, creating two triangles (each triangle will make a bag).
> 2. Roll the triangle into a cone. Fold over any extra from the top to secure the cone and keep it from unwinding.
> 3. If you have decorating tips, snip off the end of the paper cone so that the tip just fits into the cone end. Cut off more paper, if needed, to make the tip fit into the cone.
> 4. If you don't have decorating tips, simply snip off a small amount of the tip of the cone. The more you cut off, the bigger the opening.
> 5. Fill the bag with the mixture to be piped.
> 6. Bring the edges of the cone together at the top and fold them over to close the bag. Squeeze out the chocolate through the tip or end of the bag.

Cake pans - Many of the recipes in this book call for special pans like springform pans. You may be tempted to substitute other pans or different sized pans. Please do not! The times and temperatures for each recipe have been designed for the proper type and size of pan. One of the secrets for success in baking is using the right tools. Most pans can be purchased inexpensively in the houseware departments of department or variety stores. For more specialized equipment like baking rings, try kitchen stores, baking supply shops, or mail order (see Appendix I).

You may want to add the following pans/baking dishes in various sizes to your kitchen:
- ✔ Springform pans
- ✔ Square pans
- ✔ Rectangle pans
- ✔ Loaf pans
- ✔ Bundt pans
- ✔ Tart/tartlet pans
- ✔ Baking sheets
- ✔ Ring molds
- ✔ Custard/soufflé cups

Ice cream freezer - There's nothing quite like fresh, homemade ice cream on a hot summer's day and an ice cream freezer makes it possible. While hand crank ice cream freezers are a romantic idea, the romance quickly fades as the ice cream hardens and cranking becomes a chore. A better choice is an electric model. Some models require placing the freezer cylinder in the freezer compartment for several hours or overnight. They only make a small amount of ice cream (usually about a quart) and don't allow for "spur-of-the-moment" ice cream making. We think a better choice is an electric ice cream freezer that uses ice and rock salt. They're often available for $30 or less, are easy to use, and make terrific ice cream.

Parchment paper - Several of the recipes call for parchment paper. This paper is used to line baking pans and makes it easier to remove cakes from pans. Some people use waxed paper in place of parchment, but parchment paper works better. Parchment paper is usually available in the grocery section where you buy waxed paper. If it is not available at your local grocery store, try up-scale grocers, specialty food markets, bakery supply stores, or mail order.

Mixer - Most ingredients can be mixed with a whisk. However, electric appliances make it easy to create spectacular desserts with a minimum of effort. If, for instance you're making a spongecake batter with a whisk, you have to use both horizontal and vertical movements to get all the batter, including the batter that clings to the sides of the bowl, incorporated. Not an easy task. If you're using a hand mixer, it gets a bit easier, but the mixer can only mix horizontally, leaving much of the batter on the sides unmixed. A stand mixer with a moving head like a Kitchenaid or Hobart mixes the batter and rotates around the bowl, allowing the batter around the sides to run back into the mixture being beaten. Be sure to read the directions for moveable head mixers as some ingredients need less mixing time with these machines.

Ring molds - These are bottomless circles of metal. We use them to make individual warm chocolate cakes. They're available in various sizes from well-stocked kitchen stores. If you can't find them in your town, pastry chef Colin Cameron from RiverPlace Hotel in Portland, Oregon, says, "You can use any oven-proof ramekin that has straight sides. The advantage to having bottomless ring molds is easily getting the cake out when it's warm. You can make your own ring molds from small cans with the tops and bottoms cut off. For instance, for a 3 1/2 inch ring mold you can use small fruit or tomato sauce cans. For larger sizes, large tuna cans might work. At Riverplace, I use various sizes of PVC pipe cut to the size I need."

Scale - Professional pastry chefs weigh everything, including dry ingredients like flour and sugar. We've converted many of these to more conventional measurements for the home cook. However, some baking ingredients, including chocolate, require weighing. Relatively inexpensive kitchen scales can be purchased at kitchen shops.

Thermometer - Because chocolate is so temperature-sensitive, a chocolate thermometer or an Insta-Read meat thermometer is essential when cooking with chocolate.

Chocolate thermometers, available at better kitchen shops or by mail order, cover a range of 40-130 degrees Fahrenheit in one-degree increments, which allows you to temper chocolate properly.

Techniques

Adding nut garnish - How do the pros add those beautiful chopped nut finishes to their cakes and tortes? James Cecil, pastry chef at the restaurant at Awbrey Glen Golf Course in Bend, Oregon, offers these suggestions for adding a chopped nut garnish to the sides of a cake or torte. "Place a pan under the bottom of the cake to catch the falling nuts for reuse. Then, with one hand under the bottom of the cake pan, take a handful of nuts and gently press the nuts into the side of the cake. Rotate the cake as needed to finish the sides."

Chopping chocolate - On a cutting board, place a large, heavy knife or cleaver at the edge of the chocolate. Cut off small pieces evenly for melting. If you need to chop the chocolate into smaller pieces, keep the tip of the knife on the cutting surface, holding top of the blade with the flat part of your hand to hold it against the work surface. Then lift the handle of the blade slightly and move it in an arc, using the knife point as a pivot point.

Chocolate decorations - Chocolate is an excellent medium for making garnishes.
  • *Chocolate shreds -* Chill a chocolate bar. Place a grater over a plate or tray to catch the shreds. Run the chocolate over the grater, creating shreds. Clean the grater frequently to prevent clogging. If your hands are warm, use a piece of waxed paper or plastic wrap to hold the chocolate.

  • *Chocolate curls/shavings -* Pastry chef Suzanne Leech, owner of Suzanne's Specialty Baking in Bellingham, Washington, has this advice about shaving chocolate. "The trick to shaving chocolate is having it at the right temperature. Set a solid piece of chocolate at least 6 inches long in a warm place (80-95 degrees) for a few minutes or in a microwave oven for a few seconds. For ease of handling, wrap the chocolate in plastic wrap, exposing only the side you are shaving. With a vegetable peeler, peel off the chocolate. Alternate sides of the chocolate often, as your hand will warm the chocolate."

For very large chocolate curls, melt 1 1/2 ounces of semi-sweet or milk chocolate and 1 teaspoon of shortening in the top of a double boiler (see melting chocolate directions in this section), stirring to blend well. Using a spatula with an offset blade, spread thinly and evenly over the *outside* bottom of a glass baking dish. Cool until set. With a straight edge spatula, apply a steady and gentle pressure, pushing the spatula through the chocolate to make curls. Lift the curls with a wooden skewer and use immediately or place in a single layer on paper towels in a storage container until needed.

• *Chocolate drizzles* - Drizzles of melted white or dark chocolate make a beautiful addition to cookies and other desserts. Place the cookies or other items to be decorated on a wire rack over waxed paper. Dip a fork into melted chocolate and drizzle over the tops of the cookies. For a more controlled drizzle, place the melted chocolate into a pastry bag with a small tip or heavy-duty plastic bag and snip off the end (for a bigger drizzle, snip more off the end). Squeeze the bag as you move across the tops of the cookies. If the chocolate becomes too cool, reheat the bag in a microwave for 10 seconds.

• *Chocolate leaves* - Wash and dry small, nontoxic leaves like lemon, lime, mint, or rose leaves. Melt 1 1/2 ounces of chocolate and 1 teaspoon of shortening in the top of a double boiler. Stir occasionally. Use a small clean paintbrush and brush melted chocolate on the underside of each leaf. Wipe away any chocolate that gets on the top of the leaves. Place leaves chocolate side up on waxed paper until the chocolate has set. Carefully peel the leaves away from the chocolate. Use immediately or place on a single layer of waxed paper in a storage container until needed.

Cutting a cake or torte - James Cecil, pastry chef at the clubhouse restaurant at Awbrey Glen Golf Course in Bend, Oregon, says, "Place a large knife in a large container of hot water or use hot running water to heat the knife. Wipe off the water each time you cut the cake. Then re-heat under the water, wipe, and make another cut."

Making chocolate cups - These elegant cups deliciously dress up desserts like chocolate mousse. Skamania Lodge's pastry chef, Kristen Wood, shares her simple technique for making chocolate cups. Brush melted semi-sweet chocolate inside small waxed paper cups. Chill briefly and repeat with two more coats of melted chocolate in each cup. Chill between each coat.

To remove the chocolate cups from the paper cups, lightly scrape any drips of chocolate from the lip of the cups with the back of a paring knife. Then, gently press the bottom of the cup and the chocolate cup should pop right out.

Making chocolate sacks - Like chocolate cups, chocolate sacks create an elegant presentation. Chef Patricia Dickey from Whale's Tale in Newport, Oregon, tells us how they make them. To make six chocolate sacks: In the top of a double boiler, melt 1 pound of chocolate over hot, not boiling, water. Keep warm over very low heat.

Cut off the tops of six 1/2-pound plastic-coated coffee bags so they are about 2 inches high. Open the bags and keep the sides as straight as possible. Ladle about 2 table-spoons of chocolate into a bag. Dip a natural bristle paintbrush into the melted chocolate and paint the inside of the bag (sides and bottom) with the chocolate. Repeat the ladling and painting for each bag. Place the chocolate-coated bags in a large pan. Set the pan of bags in the freezer for about 10 minutes or until the chocolate is set.

Remove from freezer and give each bag a second coat of chocolate. Return to the freezer. When the second coat is set, remove the pan from the freezer. Pipe or spoon the dessert into each bag. Carefully peel the paper bags from the outside of each bag. Refrigerate until serving time.

Measuring ingredients - Baking is an exact science requiring careful weighing and measuring. To measure dry ingredients like cocoa, confectioners' sugar, and flour, lightly spoon the ingredient into the appropriate dry measuring cup and level it off with the straight edge of a knife or spatula. Do not tap the measuring cup or it will result in an inaccurate measure.

Glass or plastic cups with a spout are intended for measuring liquid ingredients. If you use a liquid measuring cup for dry ingredients like flour, you get an extra tablespoon of flour per cup, enough to make your baked goods dry and less flavorful.

Melting chocolate - The biggest mistake home cooks make with chocolate, according to veteran chefs and chocolatiers, is getting it too hot. Chocolatier Janele Smith, owner of Fenton and Lee Chocolates in Eugene, Oregon, says, "In many homes, the kitchen is too warm for working with chocolate. Then they get the chocolate too hot."

When melting or working with chocolate, there are two principles to keep in mind:
 1. Chocolate burns easily.
 2. Chocolate and water (or steam) don't mix.

To Melt Chocolate: Chop or break it into even pieces (no larger than 1 inch) to help it melt evenly. There are three ways to melt chocolate: the hot water method, the double boiler method, and the microwave method.

   1. Hot water method. Heat a pan of water to hot (not boiling) and take it off the heat. Place a metal or heat-resistant glass bowl over the pan. Make sure the bowl fits well and doesn't allow any steam to escape from the hot water. Put the chopped chocolate into the bowl and stir occasionally until melted.

   2. Double boiler method. Place the chopped chocolate in the top of a double boiler and heat the water until hot (not boiling). Remove the double boiler from the heat. When one-third of the chocolate is melted, stir slowly and often until the chocolate is completely melted. Don't heat the chocolate over 120 degrees Fahrenheit. Be careful not to allow steam from the hot water to come in contact with the chocolate.

3. Microwave method. Place chopped chocolate in a microwave-resistant bowl at 50% power. Stir the chocolate every 10-20 seconds or until the chocolate is melted.

To Melt White Chocolate: Chill the white chocolate well in the refrigerator. Then grind in a food processor before melting over a double boiler.

Use melted sweet chocolate, milk chocolate, and white chocolate immediately. Melted unsweetened and semi-sweet chocolate can kept for about 10 minutes after melting.

Preparing nuts - Nuts of all types make wonderful additions to chocolate. Nuts with skins need to have the skins removed before using. For loose-skinned nuts like almonds, you can use the **par-boiling method to remove skins.**
1. Place shelled nuts into a pan of boiling water and boil for 1 minute.
2. Use a slotted spoon or skimmer and remove nuts from pan and place in a colander.
3. Let the nuts cool slightly. Rub each nut lightly with your fingers. The skin should easily pop off.
4. To dry the nuts after par boiling, place in a single layer on a cookie sheet and bake for 5 minutes in a preheated 325 degree oven.

For nuts that have tighter skins like hazelnuts, you'll need to use the **roasting method to remove skins.**
1. Spread nuts on a baking sheet. Place in 350 degree preheated oven for about 10 minutes.
2. Place the roasted nuts on a towel. Place another towel on top of the nuts. Use your hands to roll the nuts in the towel. After a couple minutes of rubbing, most skins will be removed.
3. For stubborn skins, rub each nut between your fingers.

Rescuing "seized" chocolate - If melting chocolate suddenly becomes grainy and unworkable (seizes), it has been contaminated with water or steam. When chocolate seizes, it is not good for coating anymore, but it can be used in ganache, in batters, or in frostings if you "rescue" it. Add 1 tablespoon vegetable oil or 1 tablespoon warm water for each 2 ounces of chocolate and whisk briskly until the chocolate is smooth (be sure to subtract the amount of liquid added from the recipe). Not all chocolate responds to this "doctoring," but it's worth the effort.

Storing chocolate - Chocolate is highly susceptible to odors so it needs to be carefully wrapped in plastic wrap and stored away from strongly flavored foods. Store in a cool (60-70 degree Fahrenheit), dry, dark place. Because of the butterfat in powered milk, white chocolate will turn rancid if exposed to prolonged light.

Dark chocolate will keep for 1 year or longer. Milk chocolate and white chocolate will keep for about 5 months.

If chocolate gets too warm, the cocoa butter will separate and rise to the top, forming a whitish cast (called "bloom"). The chocolate may not look so good, but it's fine for cooking.

Tempering chocolate - Tempering chocolate is a way to make it more stable and give it a lovely sheen and snap. Anytime you're going to use chocolate for coating, the chocolate should be tempered. Products sold as dipping chocolate do not need to be tempered. However, the quality of dipping chocolate is inferior to real tempered chocolate.

Although it may take some practice at first, tempering is a relatively easy three-step process. Ideal room temperature for tempering is 65-68 degrees with low humidity.
 1. Melt the chocolate completely using one of the methods previously described. The temperature of melted chocolate should be between 115-120 degrees.
 2. Remove the chocolate from the heat source and add grated chocolate, stirring all the while. This cools the chocolate and allows the crystals in the chocolate to restructure in a more stable fashion. When the chocolate cools to about 76 degrees, it's tempered. A good way to tell if the chocolate is properly tempered is to use a spatula to smear a bit of chocolate on waxed paper. Properly tempered chocolate will harden within a couple of minutes, have a sheen to it, and snap sharply when broken.
 3. Reheat the chocolate to a working temperature (86-88 degrees for milk or white chocolate; 88-90 degrees for dark chocolate).

Temperature and Timing

All your efforts can be dashed if the temperature or timing is off on a recipe. Each of the recipes in *The Chocolate Lover's Guide Cookbook* has been tested, many of them by home cooks like yourself. However, each oven is different. Radiant, fan-assisted, or combination ovens all bake a little differently. In addition, your home oven may bake slightly hotter or cooler than the temperature indicated on the dial. It's a good idea to purchase an oven thermometer and test your oven to see if it's accurate. If it's not, have the oven serviced or make adjustments in your temperature settings.

Follow the directions and time exactly on recipes the first time. Using the right type and size pans outlined in the recipes will help ensure success. Preheat your oven to the required temperature. Note any adjustments made to time and temperature for future efforts. Also, unless otherwise specified, place pans on the middle rack of the oven for even heating.

Note that cakes with lighter batters like spongecakes require careful monitoring. For these recipes, be sure to look at the cake before it is fully baked and watch it carefully throughout the last phase of baking.

"Strength is the capacity to break a chocolate bar into four pieces with your bare hands — and then eat just one of the pieces."

— Judith Viorst

Cakes & Tortes

Rich, moist, and elegant,
cakes and tortes are among the
favorite chocolate desserts.

Suzanne's Specialty Baking, Bellingham, Washington
Chocolate Mousse Torte

This decadent torte, created by Suzanne Leech of Suzanne's Specialty Baking, is served at the wonderful Italian restaurant Il Fiasco in Bellingham, Washington. Its velvety texture and melt-in-the-mouth richness won it a Best List Award in the Best Chocolate Torte category in **The Chocolate Lover's Guide to the Pacific Northwest.**

Makes 1 9- to 10-inch torte

Bittersweet Chocolate Torte:
- 1 cup unsalted butter (2 sticks)
- 7 1/2 ounces bittersweet chocolate
- 1 1/2 ounces unsweetened chocolate
- 6 eggs, separated, divided
- 3/4 cup granulated sugar, divided
- 6 tablespoons firmly packed brown sugar
- 7 tablespoons all-purpose flour
- 1 teaspoon espresso powder
- 1/2 teaspoon cream of tartar

Rich Chocolate Mousse:
- 8 ounces bittersweet chocolate
- 4 ounces unsweetened chocolate
- 1/4 cup cold coffee or liqueur of your choice
- 2 teaspoons unflavored gelatin
- 2 1/3 cups whipping cream, divided
- 1/2 cup granulated sugar
- Shaved chocolate for garnish (see note)
- Powdered sugar for garnish

For Bittersweet Chocolate Cake: Preheat oven to 350 degrees. Line the bottom of a 9- or 10-inch springform pan with parchment paper. Grease the pan well with butter and sprinkle with flour, shaking out any excess flour.

In the top of a double boiler, melt the butter and chocolates over hot water. Stir with a whisk until smooth. Remove from heat and set aside to cool slightly while preparing remaining ingredients.

In a mixer with a whip attachment, beat the egg yolks with 1/4 cup sugar until pale and thick, about 4 minutes. Transfer yolk mixture to a clean bowl and fold in the melted chocolate.

Stir together the flour and espresso powder and sprinkle over the chocolate mixture. Fold in gently.

In the clean mixer bowl with wire whip attachment, whip the egg whites with the remaining 1/2 cup sugar until soft peaks form. Gently fold into the chocolate mixture.

Spread the batter in the prepared pan and bake for 40 to 50 minutes or until the torte has risen evenly and is still soft and jiggly in the center and beginning to crack slightly along the top edge. The torte will deflate while it cools. Wrap well and refrigerate or freeze before removing from the pan.

For Rich Chocolate Mousse: In the top of a double boiler, melt the chocolates over hot water. Stir until smooth. Remove from heat and set aside.

Stir the gelatin into the coffee and allow to sit for 5 minutes to soften. Place in pan over a hot water bath and stir until gelatin is completely dissolved. Stir into the melted chocolate.

In a small saucepan, heat 1/3 cup cream and sugar, stirring, until the sugar has dissolved. Add to the melted chocolate and whisk until smooth. Set aside to cool.

Whip the remaining 2 cups cream until soft peaks form. Fold into the cooled chocolate mixture. The mousse will be quite soft and will take several hours to set.

To Assemble the Mousse Torte: The chocolate mousse should be at room temperature. Remove the chilled chocolate torte from the springform pan. On a serving platter, spread the chocolate mousse generously over the top and sides of the torte. Garnish with shaved chocolate and powdered sugar. Refrigerate until ready to serve.

Chef's note: Due to increasing concerns about salmonella bacteria in raw eggs, the mousse in this dessert is eggless. While you sacrifice some lightness, you can make ahead and freeze both the mousse and the torte.

To shave chocolate, set a solid piece of chocolate in a warm place (80 to 95 degrees) for a few minutes or microwave for a few seconds. For ease of handling, wrap the chocolate in plastic wrap, exposing only the side you are shaving. Shave the chocolate with a vegetable peeler. As your hand will warm the chocolate, alternate sides often.

> The Amazon or Orinoco basin is believed to be the birthplace of cacao beans, the pre-cursor of chocolate.

Recipe Tester's note: You can make the chocolate torte and serve with a sprinkling of powered sugar and whipped cream and fresh berries. Or, for real chocolate fans, cover with the rich chocolate mousse.

Fountain Cafe, Port Townsend, Washington

Bittersweet Chocolate Hazelnut Torte with Raspberry Coulis

Chef Kate Harrison from the Fountain Café in Port Townsend, Washington, contributed this very dense, rich, and velvety torte. The addition of Frangelico (usually available in those airline-sized mini bottles) gives a wonderful richness. The Raspberry Coulis adds a lovely tangy sweetness.

Makes 1 8-inch torte

Bittersweet Chocolate Hazelnut Torte:
1 pound chopped bittersweet chocolate

1/2 cup plus 2 tablespoons unsalted butter

6 eggs

1 tablespoon all-purpose flour

1 cup chopped roasted hazelnuts

6 tablespoons Frangelico (hazelnut liqueur)

Raspberry Coulis:
1 12-ounce package frozen raspberries

Water

For Bittersweet Chocolate Hazelnut Torte: Preheat oven to 425 degrees. Line an 8-inch springform pan with parchment paper. Spray evenly with non-stick cooking spray.

In the top of a double boiler, melt the chocolate and butter over hot water. Set aside.

In the top of another double boiler over hot, not boiling, water whisk the eggs until they reach 120 degrees. Transfer to a mixer bowl and whip on high speed until they triple in volume. Fold flour into eggs. Fold the chocolate into the egg mixture in 3 batches. Fold in the nuts and liqueur.

Pour batter into prepared pan and bake for 10 to 12 minutes. Remove from oven and cool. Refrigerate or freeze. Make sure torte is completely cooled before cutting with a hot knife. Serve with Raspberry Coulis.

For Raspberry Coulis: Place raspberries in a small pan with enough water to barely cover. Simmer until most of the liquid has evaporated. Puree berry mixture in a blender or food processor and strain through a mesh strainer or food mill. Add a little water if sauce seems too thick.

Chef's note: This versatile torte can be frozen. If you prefer almond flavor, try Amaretto and almonds in place of the Frangelico and hazelnuts.

Just American Desserts, Spokane, Washington

Chocolate Sin

Just American Desserts, a dessert boutique in Spokane, makes dozens of delightful desserts. Once you sample Chocolate Sin, a luscious combination of chocolate, butter, eggs, and coffee, you'll know why it's their #1 seller.

Makes 1 9-inch cake

1 pound unsalted butter
1 cup plus 2 tablespoons granulated sugar
1 cup plus 2 tablespoons brewed coffee
12 ounces chopped semi-sweet chocolate
4 ounces chopped unsweetened chocolate
8 eggs
Raspberry puree for garnish
Whipped cream for garnish

Preheat oven to 350 degrees. Grease and flour a 9-inch springform pan.

In a medium saucepan over low heat, melt together the butter, sugar, and coffee. Whisk to combine well. Add chocolates and whisk until melted. Remove from heat and whisk in eggs, one at a time.

Pour into prepared pan and bake for 50-55 minutes. Cake is done when the top has formed a crust (cake should not jiggle). Cool and refrigerate. While chilled, cut into servings with a hot knife.

Serve at room temperature on a bed of raspberry sauce with a dollop of whipped cream.

Americans love chocolate. We import more cacao beans than any other country in the world.

Pacific Café, Bellingham, Washington

Chocolate Decadence

The rich, custard-like mousseline sauce makes this chocolate decadence even more special.

Makes 1 10-inch torte

Chocolate Decadence:

6 ounces sweet dark chocolate

7 ounces unsweetened chocolate

1/2 cup plus 2 tablespoons water

14 tablespoons granulated sugar, divided

1 cup plus 2 tablespoons unsalted butter, softened

6 eggs

Whipped cream for garnish

White chocolate curls for garnish

Mousseline Sauce:

Scant 1/4 cup granulated sugar

3 egg yolks

2 3/4 tablespoon boiling water

3/4 cup whipping cream

2 teaspoons vanilla

For Chocolate Decadence: Preheat oven to 350 degrees. Brush a 10 by 2-inch round cake pan with melted butter. Line bottom with parchment paper and brush with melted butter.

Chop chocolate into small pieces and mix together.

In a medium saucepan, bring water and 7 tablespoons sugar to a boil. Add chocolate and stir until melted and smooth. Cut butter into chunks and add to chocolate mixture, stirring until melted and incorporated. Set aside.

In a large mixing bowl, on high speed, whip eggs and remaining 7 tablespoons sugar for 3 minutes or until light and very fluffy. Gently fold warm, but not hot, chocolate into the egg mixture.

Pour into the prepared pan. Place the filled cake pan into a larger baking pan and add boiling water to the larger pan until it reaches half way up the sides of the cake pan. (If using a springform pan, line the bottom and sides with heavy duty aluminum foil before placing in water bath.) Bake for about 50 minutes or until the top feels firm. Cool.

Refrigerate, covered, for at least 2 hours or overnight. Cake must be completely set before unmolding.

To unmold, briefly warm the bottom of the cake pan over gas or electric burner until cake moves freely from sides of the pan. (Or dip bottom and sides of the pan briefly in hot water.) Invert cake onto a cardboard circle or serving platter. Peel off paper. Garnish with whipped cream florets and white chocolate curls. Serve with Mousseline Sauce on the side.

For Mousseline Sauce: Combine the sugar and egg yolks in a large mixing bowl. Whisk to combine and then whip in boiling water. Place the bowl over simmering water and cook, whipping constantly, until the eggs are very thick and pale. The mixture should fall slowly off the beaters in a ribbonlike pattern and, after a few seconds, sink back into the batter. Remove from heat and whip until cool.

Whip cream and vanilla to a saucelike consistency. Gently fold the cream into the egg mixture until well combined. Refrigerate until needed.

> The word "chocolate" comes from a combination of the Mayan word "xocoatl" and the Aztec word for cocoa, "cacahuatl" meaning "food of the gods."

Ship Bay Oyster House, Eastsound, Washington

Chocolate Hazelnut Torte

Pat Andrews, owner of Ship Bay Oyster House, shares her recipe for the restaurant's signature Chocolate Hazelnut Torte. This dessert delightfully combines the silky richness of semi-sweet chocolate and the nutty goodness of roasted hazelnuts. Our tester tells us this is a no-fault recipe that will impress your guests.

Makes 1 9-inch torte

Cake:
6 ounces semi-sweet chocolate chips
1 1/2 cups roasted hazelnuts
3/4 cups granulated sugar, divided
3/4 cup unsalted butter
6 eggs, separated
1/8 teaspoon salt
1 teaspoon fresh lemon juice

Icing:
1/2 cups whipping cream
8 ounces semi-sweet chocolate chips
1 tablespoon unsalted butter

For Cake: Preheat oven to 350 degrees. Spray a 9-inch springform pan with non-stick spray.

Place the chocolate chips in the top of a double boiler and melt over warm water on medium heat. Cover until partially melted, then remove cover and stir until melted and smooth. Remove from double boiler and set aside until room temperature.

Place hazelnuts and 1/4 cup sugar in the bowl of a food processor and process until finely ground (almost powdery). Stop the machine once or twice and scrape down the sides of the bowl. Process for at least one full minute. Set aside.

In the large bowl of an electric mixer, cream the butter. Add 1/4 cup sugar and cream until light and fluffy. Add the egg yolks, one at a time, beating and scraping the bowl until well incorporated. On low speed, add the chocolate and beat until well mixed. Add the processed hazelnuts and mix well.

Whip the egg whites in a clean bowl of an electric mixer with the salt and lemon juice. Start beating on low speed and increase speed gradually. When the

> During the 12th century in the area that now occupies central Mexico and Central America, people shared a mug of frothy chocolate as part of the marriage ceremony.

whites hold soft peaks, gradually add the remaining 1/4 cup sugar. Then beat at high speed until the whites hold stiff peaks.

Stir a large spoonful of the whites into the chocolate mixture to soften, then fold in the remaining whites in three additions.

Pour the batter into the prepared pan and bake for 60-70 minutes. Do not over bake. Cake will be moist, but the top will be slightly dry. Cool on a rack before icing.

For Icing: Combine cream, chocolate chips, and butter in the top of a double boiler. Melt over hot water until the chocolate is just melted. Stir until smooth. Pour icing over the cake and rotate pan to cover top. Decorate, if desired, with chopped hazelnuts or chocolate shavings.

Oyster Creek Inn, Bow, Washington

Chocolate Decadence with Orange Crème Anglaise

This Chocolate Decadence has a delicate, cake-like texture with a deep chocolate flavor. The Crème Anglaise is light yet rich with the refreshing lilt of orange.

Makes 1 8-inch cake

Chocolate Decadence:
- 12 ounces chopped semi-sweet chocolate
- 12 ounces chopped milk chocolate
- 3/4 cup plus 3 tablespoons butter
- 6 eggs
- 1 1/2 teaspoons vanilla
- 1 1/2 tablespoons granulated sugar
- 1 1/2 teaspoons all-purpose flour

Orange Crème Anglaise:
- 1 cup whipping cream
- 3 egg yolks
- 1/4 cup granulated sugar
- 1 tablespoon Triple Sec
- 1 teaspoon grated orange peel

For Chocolate Decadence: Preheat oven to 400 degrees. Line an 8-inch cake pan with aluminum foil, bringing foil up the sides of the pan.

In the top of a double boiler, melt the chocolates and butter over hot water. Stir until well blended.

In a large bowl of an electric mixer, beat the eggs with the vanilla. Sprinkle in the sugar and beat until very pale and tripled in volume. Sprinkle the flour over the eggs and continue beating until well combined. Fold the chocolate into the egg mixture.

Pour the batter into the prepared pan and bake for 24 minutes. Do not over bake.

Cool to room temperature and then chill in the refrigerator. Cut into wedges with a hot knife. Serve at room temperature with Orange Crème Anglaise.

For Orange Crème Anglaise: In a small saucepan, bring the cream to a simmer. Do not boil.

While the cream is heating, whip the egg yolks with the sugar until the mixture is very thick and pale and forms a ribbon-like pattern when the beaters are lifted out of the batter. Slowly add the egg mixture to the hot cream, whisking over low heat until the mixture coats the back of a spoon, about 10 minutes. Whisk in Triple Sec and orange peel. Remove from heat and pour into a cool bowl. Refrigerate until ready to use.

Chef's note: When in doubt, underbake!

Actress Melina Kanakaredes, who plays Dr. Sydney Hansen on the hit TV show "Providence," says her family owns a chocolate store and she was raised on chocolate. When she visits the family store, she "becomes a 3-year-old again, cutting a chunk of chocolate and rolling it in chopped nuts. It's my own personal Willy Wonka factory."
— Parade magazine

Chocolate Velvet Decadence Torte

This torte, from the beautiful Awbrey Glen Country Club situated outside of Bend in wilds of central Oregon, is a chocolate lover's delight. This recipe from chef James Cecil requires time to let each step cool before assembling.

Makes 1 10-inch torte

Crust:

1 cup chocolate cookie crumbs

1/4 cup melted butter

Torte:

1 1/2 pounds chopped bittersweet or dark chocolate

1/2 cup strong brewed coffee

1/2 cup Grand Marnier

3 eggs, separated

1 cup whipping cream

Garnish:

1/2 cup melted white chocolate

1 1/2 cups chopped hazelnuts

For Crust: Preheat oven to 350 degrees.

Stir together the cookie crumbs and butter. Press onto the bottom of a 10-inch springform pan. Bake for 8 to 10 minutes or until firm. Cool on a wire rack. Set aside.

For Torte: In the top of a double boiler, melt the chocolate over simmering water. When the chocolate is melted, stir in the coffee and Grand Marnier. Add the egg yolks and mix well. Remove from heat and set aside to cool.

Whip the cream until firm peaks form.

Whip the egg whites until stiff peaks form. Working quickly, fold the whipped cream and then the egg whites into the warm chocolate mixture. Pour batter into baked crust and spread evenly. Chill for 1 to 2 hours.

To serve, carefully remove sides of springform pan. Fill a pastry bag fitted with a small plain tip with melted white chocolate. Pipe chocolate stripes over top of torte. Turn torte 180 degrees and pipe stripes in a criss cross pattern. With one hand under the bottom of the torte, gently place nuts on the side of the torte.

Cut into 12 to 16 servings with a hot dry knife. Chill until ready to serve.

Note: See raw egg caution, page 18.

Fran's Chocolates, Seattle and Bellevue, Washington

Triple Chocolate Cake

The Chocolate Lover's Guide to the Pacific Northwest named Fran Bigelow Best *Chocolatier in the Pacific Northwest. Here Fran shares her rich, classic Triple Chocolate Cake.*

Makes 12-16 servings

Chocolate Sponge Cake:

3/4 cup butter (1 1/2 sticks)

3/4 cup sugar

8 ounces almond paste

2/3 cup unsweetened cocoa powder

4 eggs

Three Chocolate Filling:

6 ounces milk chocolate with finely ground hazelnuts (gianduja)

(or substitute 4 ounces milk chocolate and 2 ounces hazelnut paste)

4 ounces milk chocolate

3 ounces semi-sweet chocolate

1 cup butter (2 sticks)

Glaze:

3/4 cup cream

8 ounces semi-sweet chocolate, chopped

For Chocolate Cake: Preheat oven to 350 degrees. Line a jelly-roll pan (10 x 14) with parchment paper.

In a bowl, cream butter and sugar until fluffy. Add almond paste. Beat until smooth. Add eggs slowly. Fold in cocoa. Pour into prepared pan. Bake 10-12 minutes or until done. When cool, remove from pan and peel off parchment paper.

For Filling: Melt chocolates over low heat over a water bath. Cool slightly (about 95 degrees). In the bowl of a mixer, cream butter using the paddle. Slowly add chocolates making sure butter does not melt.

For Glaze: Bring cream to a boil. Add chopped chocolate. Stir until smooth. Cool.

Assembly: Divide cake into thirds, cutting into approximately 4 1/2-inch strips. Spread one-third of the filling on a section. Place one section on top of the filled one. Add a layer of filling, then place the third strip on top. Spread filling on sides and edges of cake. Refrigerate.

When cake is completely cool, place cake on rack. Pour glaze over top using a spatula to spread and smooth it.

Black Butte Ranch Dining Room, Black Butte, Oregon

Sourdough Chocolate Cake

This cake, the signature dessert at Black Butte Ranch, was developed by the restaurant's former pastry chef, Alta Brockett. It's rich and warm without being too heavy. You'll need to allow 2-3 hours to let the sourdough starter "ripen" before proceeding with this recipe.

Makes one 9-inch cake

       1/2 cup thick sourdough starter

       1/4 cup non fat dry milk

       1 cup warm water

       1 1/2 cups all-purpose flour

       1/2 cup unsweetened cocoa powder

       1 cup granulated sugar

       1/2 cup shortening

       1/2 teaspoon baking soda

       1 teaspoon vanilla

       1 teaspoon cinnamon

       2 eggs

       Mocha icing

Stir together the sourdough starter, dry milk, water, flour, and cocoa. Let stand in a warm place for 2 to 3 hours or until the mixture smells yeasty.

Preheat the oven to 350 degrees. Grease and flour a 9 by 13-inch baking pan.

Cream together the sugar, shortening, salt, soda, vanilla, and cinnamon. Add the eggs one at a time, beating well after each addition. Add the creamed mixture to the sourdough mixture. Mix on low speed of mixer for 1 to 2 minutes.

Pour into prepared pan and bake for 25 to 30 minutes or until toothpick inserted in top of cake comes out clean. Cool on wire rack and frost with mocha icing.

Mocha Icing

       5 tablespoons butter, room temperature

       3 tablespoons cocoa

       2 1/2 cups powdered sugar

       3 tablespoons strong black coffee (or 2 teaspoons instant coffee and 3 table-
          spoons water)

       1 teaspoon vanilla

Cream butter, add cocoa and mix well. Add sugar alternately with coffee. Add vanilla and mix well. Add more sugar, if necessary. Frost sourdough chocolate cake.

Serve warm (1 minute on high in the microwave for each piece) with a scoop of vanilla ice cream.

Genoa, Portland, Oregon
Torta di Santa Maria

*Genoa, a popular pre-fixe Italian restaurant in Portland, Oregon, has been delighting din-
ers for more than 25 years. This unusual torta, packed with raisins, hazelnuts, and the sweet
flavor of orange, is one of the restaurant's signature desserts.*

Makes 1 8-inch torta

Torta:

1/2 cup butter

2/3 cup granulated sugar

3 eggs

3/4 cup raisins soaked in orange liqueur

1 cup ground hazelnuts

3/4 cup bittersweet chocolate chips, melted

1/4 cup breadcrumbs

Grated peel of 1 orange

Glaze:

4 ounces semi-sweet chocolate

1 ounce unsweetened chocolate

4 tablespoons butter, softened

2 tablespoons brewed espresso
coffee

For Torta: Preheat oven to 375 degrees. Butter an 8-inch cake pan. Line the buttered pan
with parchment paper and butter the paper.

Cream the butter with the sugar. Add the eggs,
one at a time, beating well after each addition. Stir in
the raisins, hazelnuts, chocolate, breadcrumbs, and orange peel.

Turn into the prepared pan and bake for 30 minutes. Cool.

Pour prepared glaze over torta and tilt to cover
smoothly. Let stand to set.

For Glaze: Melt the chocolate in the top of a double
boiler over hot water. When chocolate is completely
melted, whisk in softened butter and espresso. Cool
slightly until the glaze is a good pouring consistency.

> Dogs love chocolate,
> but it can be deadly for
> them. The chocolate
> ingredient, theobromine,
> stimulates the heart and
> nervous system and can
> cause a dog's heart to
> overbeat.

The Wayfarer Restaurant, Cannon Beach, Oregon
Chocolate Ganache Torte

The Wayfarer Restaurant won second place in Seaview's Chocolate Festival with this Ganache Torte. The nutty crust provides a crunchy contrast to the smooth chocolate.

Makes 12 servings

Crust:
3 cups pecans

1/3 cup granulated sugar

1/3 cup melted butter

Filling:
2 2/3 cup whipping cream

1 1/2 pounds chopped semi-sweet chocolate

1 egg yolk

Caramel Sauce:
1/2 cup granulated sugar

1/2 cup plus 3 tablespoons light corn syrup

2 tablespoons water

1/4 cup whipping cream

1/2 cup butter

Sweetened whipped cream for garnish

For Crust: Preheat oven to 350 degrees. Lightly butter the bottom of a 10-inch springform pan.

Place the pecans in the bowl of a food processor and pulse to chop. With the processor running, slowly add the sugar and then pour in the butter. Process just until butter is incorporated.

Pat the crust onto the bottom of the prepared pan. Bake for about 10 minutes or until brown. Set aside on wire rack to cool.

For Filling: Heat the cream in a small saucepan until tiny bubbles form around the edges of the pan.

Place the chopped chocolate in a large bowl and pour the hot cream over. Stir until the chocolate is melted and the mixture is blended. Whisk in the egg yolk. Pour into cooled crust and chill until firm.

For Caramel Sauce: Combine the sugar, corn syrup, and water in a heavy-bottomed saucepan. Cook over medium to medium-high heat until the sauce is a light caramel color. Cover the pan for the first 30 seconds to dissolve any sugar crystals on the sides of the pan. Remove cover and do not stir while boiling the caramel sauce.

When caramel sauce is the right color, remove from heat and stir in butter and cream. Cool.

To Serve: Cut the torte into 12 equal portions using a hot, dry knife. Garnish each serving with a drizzle of caramel sauce and whipped cream, if desired.

Note: See raw egg caution, page 18.

To raise money during the 17th century, the English government imposed high taxes on raw cacao beans. If you were caught trying to smuggle chocolate and avoid paying the taxes, you could be jailed for up to one year.

Canlis' Chocolate Lava Cake

The folks at Canlis call this luscious warm cake a "controlled disaster." The outside of the cake must be baked before the inside has set. The secret is to chill the batter in its baking dish before baking.

Makes 6 to 12 servings

> 1 pound chopped bittersweet chocolate
> 1 cup butter (2 sticks)
> 4 medium egg whites (1/2 cup)
> 1/2 teaspoon salt
> 1/2 teaspoon vinegar
> 1/3 cup granulated sugar
> 8 medium egg yolks (1/2 cup)
> 1 cup whipping cream
> 2 tablespoons powdered sugar
> Mint leaves for garnish
> Strawberries for garnish
> Chocolate fans for garnish

Butter 6 8-ounce soufflé cups or 12 4-ounce disposable aluminum baking cups. Arrange buttered dishes on a baking sheet and refrigerate.

In the top of a double boiler, melt the chocolate and butter over barely simmering water.

In a clean dry mixing bowl, whip the egg whites with the salt and vinegar until soft peaks form. Gradually add the sugar and continue whipping until stiff peaks form. Set aside.

Stir the egg yolks into the chocolate mixture and then fold the egg whites into the chocolate mixture. Transfer batter to a pastry bag fitted with a large plain tip and promptly pipe the batter into the chilled cups. Refrigerate filled cups for at least one hour.

> Casanova, the famous Italian lover, is said to have used chocolate to seduce his lovers.

Shortly before baking, preheat oven to 350 degrees. Bake 4-ounce cakes for 10 minutes and 8-ounce cakes for 18 minutes. Cakes are done when tops are crackly but insides are not set.

While cakes are baking, whip cream with powdered sugar until soft peaks form. Refrigerate until needed as a garnish.

To serve, invert each warm cake onto a plate and garnish with a dollop of whipped cream, a strawberry, a mint leaf, and a chocolate fan.

Lord Bennett's, Bandon, Oregon
Chocolate Hazelnut Cake

This cake has a brownie-like texture and a smooth, rich flavor. The icing has a lovely creamy texture.

Makes 1 8-inch cake

Cake:
> 4 eggs, separated
> 1 1/4 cups granulated sugar
> 5 ounces unsweetened chocolate
> 3/4 cup unsalted butter (1 1/2 sticks)
> 1 cup plus 1 tablespoon cake flour
> 1/4 teaspoon salt
> 4 tablespoons finely ground toasted skinned hazelnuts

Icing:
> 1 1/2 cups whipping cream
> 2 teaspoons vanilla
> 1/3 cup unsweetened cocoa powder
> 1 1/2 cup powdered sugar
> 1 teaspoon instant espresso powder
> 8 whole hazelnuts for garnish

For Cake: Preheat oven to 350 degrees. Grease an 8-inch springform pan. Line the bottom of the pan with waxed paper or parchment paper. Grease and flour the paper and sides of the pan, shaking out any excess flour.

In a large mixing bowl, whip the egg yolks and sugar together until pale and thick.

In the top of a double boiler, melt the chocolate and butter over hot water, whisking until smooth. Let mixture cool slightly. When cooled, stir the chocolate mixture into the egg yolks.

Stir together the flour, salt, and ground hazelnuts. Add to the chocolate and egg yolk mixture and stir to blend well.

In a large mixing bowl, whip the egg whites until stiff, but not dry, peaks form. Fold the egg whites into the chocolate batter, being careful not to deflate the egg whites too much.

Pour the batter into the prepared pan and bake for 35-40 minutes or until the cake tests done. Cool slightly and remove from pan. Cool on wire rack.

For Icing: In a medium bowl, stir together the cream, vanilla, cocoa powder, powdered sugar, and espresso powder. Blend well and pour over cooled cake. Set aside until icing is set and then garnish with whole hazelnuts.

Flying Fish, Seattle, Washington

Grappa Brownie Cake

This is a rich, fudgy dessert. The top is slightly crusty and the center is rich and gooey.

Makes 6 servings

Chocolate Batter:

4 ounces chopped bittersweet chocolate

1 1/4 ounces chopped semi-sweet chocolate

1/2 cup unsalted butter (1 stick)

2 tablespoons cornstarch

3/4 cup granulated sugar

3 eggs

3 egg yolks

1 1/2 teaspoons grappa

Chocolate Shortbread:

3/4 cup plus 2 tablespoons unsalted butter

1/4 cup granulated sugar

1 small egg

1/2 teaspoon vanilla

1 cup plus 1 tablespoon all-purpose flour

1 1/2 tablespoons unsweetened cocoa powder

Assembly:

6 1 1/4-ounce pieces white chocolate

6 6 by 4-inch pastry rings * (see note p. 22)

Sweetened whipped cream for garnish

Chocolate sauce for garnish

For Chocolate Batter: In the top of a double boiler, melt the chocolates and butter over simmering water. Stir to blend well. Do not over heat. Set aside to cool.

Whisk together the cornstarch and sugar. Add to the melted chocolate and whisk to combine.

Whisk the eggs and egg yolks together. Add the eggs along with the grappa to the melted chocolate mixture. Whisk until smooth. Cover and refrigerate overnight.

For Shortbread: Cream the butter with the sugar until light and fluffy. Add the egg and vanilla and mix well.

Sift the flour with the cocoa powder. Add to creamed mixture and stir until just combined.

Place dough on parchment lined baking sheet and pat out as flat as possible. Cover and refrigerate overnight.

To Assemble: Preheat oven to 350 degrees. Spray pastry rings with non-stick spray. Line a large baking sheet with parchment paper.

On a lightly floured surface, roll out the shortbread dough to 1/4-inch thick. Using the pastry rings as cookie cutters, cut out 6 chocolate rounds. Place each round on the lined baking sheet with the pastry ring set in place over the dough.

Divide the chocolate batter into two equal portions. Divide the first batch of chocolate batter equally between the pastry rings. Place a piece of white chocolate in each ring. Fill the rings with equal amounts of the second batch of batter.

Bake for 40 to 45 minutes or until the tops begin to crack. Turn the baking sheet around halfway through baking.

Serve the cakes warm with whipped cream and chocolate sauce.

Joan Steuer, editor of *Chocolatier* magazine, says 98% of people in the United States love chocolate. The other 2%, she claims, "are either allergic or won't admit it because they're closet chocophiles."

Chocolate Oblivion Torte

This easy-to-make recipe is a real crowd-pleaser. Our tester tried it out at a large party and got rave reviews.

Makes 1 8-inch torte
Torte:
> 1 pound chopped bittersweet chocolate
> 1 cup butter (2 sticks)
> 6 eggs

Ganache:
> 1 pound chopped semi-sweet chocolate
> 1/4 cup butter, softened
> 1/4 cup whipping cream

For Torte: Preheat oven to 325 degrees. Line an 8-inch springform pan with parchment paper and then spray with non-stick spray. Wrap the outside of the pan with 2 layers of aluminum foil to make the pan watertight.

In the top of a double boiler, melt the chocolate and butter over hot water. Whisk until smooth and cool slightly.

Whip the eggs with an electric mixer until pale and thick. Fold the cooled chocolate mixture into the eggs.

Pour the chocolate mixture into the prepared springform pan and place the springform pan into a larger baking pan. Pour boiling water into the larger pan until the water comes about halfway up the sides of the springform pan. Bake for 20 minutes. The torte will be heated through but liquid in the center. It will set up as it cools. Cool the torte for 4 hours at room temperature or 2 hours in the refrigerator or 1 hour in the freezer.

When the torte is firm, remove the springform sides and frost with ganache.

> It can take up to 72 hours to blend (conch) high-quality milk chocolate. Less expensive, assembly-line chocolates take less than 10 minutes to blend.

For Ganache: In the top of a double boiler, melt the chocolate over hot water. Cool slightly. Stir in the butter and cream until smooth. Cool to spreading consistency.

Recipe Tester's note: This dessert is best served at room temperature so it remains soft and creamy.

Note: See raw egg caution, page 18.

Chocolate Decadence

This dense, fudge-like decadence, offered by Skamania Lodge's pastry chef, Kristin Wood, is a chocolate lover's delight.

Makes 1 8-inch cake

Cake:

1 pound chopped bittersweet chocolate

1/2 cup butter (1 stick)

1/4 cup whipping cream

1/2 teaspoon vanilla

4 tablespoons plus 2 teaspoons granulated sugar

4 eggs

1/4 cup cake flour

Garnish:

4 ounces chopped chocolate

1/2 cup whipping cream

Sweetened whipped cream for garnish

For Cake: Preheat oven to 350 degrees. Butter an 8-inch cake pan and line the bottom with parchment paper.

In the top of a double boiler, melt the chocolate with the butter, vanilla, and cream over hot water. Stir occasionally.

In the bowl of an electric mixer, whip the sugar and eggs until light and fluffy.

Sift the flour into the egg mixture with the mixer running on medium speed. Let the mixer run for a few seconds until the flour is totally incorporated.

When the chocolate is completely melted, gently fold it into the egg mixture until you have a smooth glossy batter.

Pour the batter into the prepared pan, smoothing the top with an offset spatula. Bake for 25 minutes. Remove from oven and let cool on a wire rack. The cake will fall a bit as it cools.

When the cake has cooled, remove it from the pan and wrap and freeze for several hours.

For Garnish: In the top of a double boiler, melt the chocolate and cream together. Stir until well combined. Pour over frozen cake. (Returning frosted cake to freezer for a few minutes lets the ganache set up quickly.)

To serve, cut into 24 small wedges and serve each with a dollop of whipped cream.

Teahouse Restaurant at Ferguson Point, Vancouver, British Columbia

Torta Milano

Pastry chef Benjamin de Vries shares his signature dessert from the Teahouse Restaurant in Vancouver, British Columbia. It requires a bit of work to make three separate mousses. The result is incredibly light, with the rich marriage of almond and chocolate flavors.

Makes 1 9-inch cake

Amaretti Crust:
- 1 1/2 cups blanched almonds
- 2/3 cup powdered sugar
- 2 1/4 teaspoons cornstarch
- 1/3 cup egg whites (about 2 1/2 whites)
- 1/2 cup granulated sugar
- 1/2 teaspoon almond extract
- 1/4 cup melted butter

Mascarpone Mousse:
- 2 egg yolks
- 36 tablespoons granulated sugar
- 6 tablespoons mascarpone cheese
- 1/2 envelope unflavored gelatin
- 1 tablespoon plus 1 teaspoon lemon juice
- 1/4 teaspoon almond extract
- 2/3 cup whipping cream

Milk Chocolate Mousse:
- 5 3/4 ounces chopped milk chocolate
- 1 1/4 cups whipping cream

Dark Chocolate Mousse:
- 5 3/4 ounces chopped dark chocolate
- 1 1/4 cups whipping cream

Chocolate Glaze:
- 5 1/4 ounces chopped dark chocolate
- 2/3 cup whipping cream

For Amaretti Crust: Preheat oven to 300 degrees. Line baking sheet with parchment paper.

Combine the almonds, powdered sugar, and cornstarch in the bowl of a food processor. Process until almonds are finely ground.

In a large bowl, whip the egg whites until foamy. Gradually add the sugar and continue whipping until soft peaks form. Fold the almond mixture and almond extract into the egg whites.

Using a pastry bag with a plain tip, pipe the egg white mixture onto the parchment in small dollops. Bake for 30 to 40 minutes. Remove from oven and cool completely.

Increase oven temperature to 325 degrees.

When cookies are cool, place in the bowl of a food processor and process until the cookies are pulverized. Stir in melted butter and press onto the bottom of a 9-inch cake pan. Bake for about 10 minutes or until lightly browned and set. Cool.

For Mascarpone Mousse: In a medium bowl, whip the egg yolks with the sugar until thick and pale. Stir in the mascarpone until just blended.

Soak the gelatin in 1 tablespoon water for 5 minutes. Add the softened gelatin to the lemon juice and heat over low heat until the gelatin is melted. Stir into the mascarpone mixture along with the almond extract.

In a chilled bowl, whip the cream until soft peaks form. Fold the whipped cream into the mascarpone mixture and refrigerate until needed.

For Milk Chocolate Mousse: In the top of a double boiler, melt the chocolate over warm water.

Whip the cream until thickened slightly, it should form a ribbon when the beaters are lifted from the cream. Pour into the warm chocolate and whisk vigorously until well blended. Set aside.

For Dark Chocolate Mousse: In the top of a double boiler, melt the chocolate over warm water.

Whip the cream until thickened slightly, it should form a ribbon when the beaters are lifted from the cream. Pour into the warm chocolate and whisk vigorously until well blended. Set aside.

> In 1528, the explorer Cortez wrote of the Indian chocolate beverage, "A cup of this precious beverage permits a man to walk an entire day without food."

For Glaze: Place the chopped chocolate in a small bowl. Bring the cream to a boil and pour over the chocolate. Stir until smooth and shiny.

To Assemble: Pour the milk chocolate mousse into the crust. Add the dark chocolate mousse and swirl the two together.

Put the mascarpone mousse into a pastry bag fitted with a plain tip. Pipe onto the chocolate mousse in a circular motion. Level the top and freeze to set.

Pour the glaze over the frozen cake and spread to cover evenly. Return to freezer.

Note: See raw egg caution, page 18.

ARR Place, Newport, Oregon
Mocha Torte

This torte has a wonderfully creamy texture. The coffee doesn't overwhelm, but adds to the richness.

Makes 1 9-inch torte

> 1 pound unsalted butter, room temperature
> 1 cup granulated sugar
> Pinch salt
> 18 ounces chopped bittersweet chocolate
> 1 cup strong brewed coffee
> 8 eggs
> Sweetened whipped cream for garnish

Preheat oven to 350 degrees. Butter a 9-inch springform pan and wrap the outside of the pan with aluminum foil.

In a large saucepan, combine the butter, sugar, salt, chocolate, and coffee. Heat on low heat until the chocolate is melted, stirring occasionally. When the mixture is smooth remove from heat and let cool slightly.

Place the eggs in a large mixer bowl. Whip eggs until thick and lemon-colored. When eggs are ready, pour the chocolate mixture into the eggs in a slow, steady stream with the mixer running on medium speed. Beat just until the batter is a uniform color.

Pour the batter into the prepared springform pan. Place the springform pan into a larger pan and pour boiling water into the larger pan until it comes halfway up the sides of the springform pan. Bake for 50 to 60 minutes or until a toothpick inserted in the center of the cake comes out just slightly moist. Remove from oven and cool to room temperature. Chill for 1 to 2 hours.

To serve, cut into wedges using a hot dry knife and garnish with whipped cream.

Truffle Cake

Jon Hamlin, owner and chef of Tidal Raves in Depoe Bay, shares his incredibly silky and easy-to-make truffle cake. This recipe requires considerable time to bake and cool the cake, but it's definitely worth the wait.

Makes 1 9-inch cake

1 pound chopped bittersweet or semi-sweet chocolate
1 cup butter (2 sticks)
2 1/3 cups powdered sugar (1/2 pound)
8 lightly beaten eggs

Preheat oven to 225 degrees. Lightly butter a 9-inch springform pan.

In the top of a double boiler, melt the chocolate and butter. Stir until smooth.

Remove from heat and stir in powdered sugar and eggs. When well blended, pour batter into prepared pan. Tap firmly on a counter or other hard surface to remove excess air bubbles.

Place in the middle of the preheated oven and bake for 75 minutes. Turn the oven off and allow to sit without opening the door for another 60 minutes. These times and temperatures may vary from oven to oven. You want a very smooth top surface on a cake that is firm through to the center. If the temperature is too high it will cause the cake to rise slightly like a soufflé and not be as dense.

Chill before cutting with a hot dry knife. Serve with vanilla or raspberry citrus sauce, roasted hazelnuts, or raspberry wine.

> Napoleon knew how to get a bit of quick energy. He carried chocolate on all his military campaigns.

Il Terrazzo Carmine, Seattle, Washington

Chocolate Decadence Cake

This rich decadence is a signature dessert for the well-respected Seattle restaurant, Il Terrazzo Carmine.

Makes 1 9-inch cake

1 1/3 cups granulated sugar, divided
7 tablespoons water
12 ounces chopped semi-sweet chocolate
1 cup unsalted butter (2 sticks)
5 eggs

Preheat oven to 350 degrees. Line a 9-inch cake pan with parchment paper.

In a large saucepan, combine 1 cup sugar and the water. Bring to a boil. When the sugar is dissolved stir in the chocolate and butter.

In a mixing bowl, whip the eggs with the remaining 1/3 cup sugar until they are light and creamy. Fold the egg mixture into the chocolate mixture.

Pour the batter into the prepared pan. Place the cake pan into a larger baking pan and pour boiling water around the cake pan until the water reaches half way up the sides of the cake pan. Bake for 30 minutes. Remove from oven and cool overnight.

> Chocolate is the only food that melts at the same temperature as the human body.

Campagne's Warm Chocolate Torte

This is a heavenly dessert—warm, slightly crispy on the outside, rich and gooey on the inside. Campagne's Cinnamon Ice Cream, served on the side, is the perfect complement for this elegant and delicious dessert.

Makes 8 servings

> 12 ounces chopped bittersweet chocolate
> 6 ounces chopped unsweetened chocolate
> 3/4 cup plus 2 tablespoons unsalted butter
> 5 ounces hazelnut paste (see note)
> 1/4 cup Chambord (raspberry liqueur), optional
> 8 eggs
> 8 egg yolks
> 3 cups granulated sugar
> 1/3 cup sifted cornstarch
> Cinnamon Ice Cream (see recipe page 164)

In the top of a double boiler, melt the chocolates and butter over hot water set on low heat. Stir until smooth.

When chocolate is melted whisk in hazelnut paste and Chambord.

In the bowl of a large stand mixer with wire whip attachment, beat the eggs and egg yolks on medium speed. Sift together the sugar and cornstarch. Slowly add the sugar and cornstarch to the eggs and continue whipping until the mixture is light in color and tripled in volume. Fold the egg mixture into the chocolate mixture.

Strain the entire mixture into a plastic container and refrigerate for at least 4 hours or overnight.

Preheat oven to 350 degrees. Prepare 8 3 1/2-inch ring molds by wrapping the bottoms with aluminum foil and liberally oiling the insides of the molds. (See note about ring molds and substitutes for ring molds on page 22.)

Place the ring molds on a baking sheet and, using an ice cream scoop or large spoon, fill the molds 3/4 full.

Bake for 20 to 30 minutes, turning the baking pan after 10 minutes to ensure even baking.

The tortes are done when they dome in the center and lightly crack on the top. The centers will be liquid at this point. Allow the tortes to cool for 20 minutes.

Place the rings in the center of 8 serving plates and gently remove ring. The tortes should slide easily onto the plates, but if necessary, run a paring knife around the inside edge of the torte to release. Serve immediately with Cinnamon Ice Cream.

Chef's note: Hazelnut paste (otherwise known as hazelnut butter) is available at fine specialty food store. If unavailable, substitute an equal amount of unsalted butter.

Georgia's Chocolate Cake

Georgia's is the bakery in the quaint, flower-filled town of La Conner, Washington. Locals crowd the shop in the mornings for scones, croissants, breads, and cookies. Georgia's elegant signature cake features rich ganache and fresh strawberries.

Makes 1 9-inch cake

Cake:

1 cup unsweetened cocoa powder

1 3/4 cups boiling water

1 cup unsalted butter (2 sticks)

2 1/2 cups firmly packed brown sugar

4 eggs

1 tablespoon vanilla

2 3/4 cups all-purpose flour

2 teaspoons baking soda

1/2 teaspoon baking powder

1/2 teaspoon salt

Ganache:

1/2 cup whipping cream

12 ounces chopped dark chocolate

Buttercream:

1 pound unsalted butter, room temperature

1 1/2 cups dark chocolate ganache, cooled (recipe above)

1/4 cup very strong brewed coffee or espresso

1 teaspoon vanilla

Filling:

1/2 cup whipping cream

1 heaping teaspoon instant vanilla pudding mix, optional

1 cup fresh strawberries or raspberries

For Cake: Preheat the oven to 350 degrees. Grease and flour 3 9-inch cake pans.

In a small bowl, combine the cocoa powder and boiling water, stir well. Cool to room temperature.

In a large bowl, cream the butter with the brown sugar until light and fluffy. Add the eggs, one at a time, beating well after each addition. Stir in the vanilla.

Sift together the flour, baking soda, baking powder, and salt. Add the flour to the butter mixture alternately with the cocoa mixture, beginning and ending with the flour mixture.

Pour into prepared pans and bake for 25 minutes or until cakes test done. Cool in pans for 10 minutes, loosen edges with a knife and remove from pans. Cool on wire racks.

For Ganache: Scald cream by heating in a small saucepan until tiny bubbles form around the edges. Pour hot cream over chopped chocolate in a small bowl and stir until chocolate is melted and mixture is smooth. Cool completely.

For Buttercream: Whip the butter in a mixer at high speed for 5 minutes or until the butter turns almost white. Scrape down the sides of the bowl while whipping. Add ganache in thirds, whipping for 2 minutes on high speed after each addition. Add coffee and vanilla and whip another 2 minutes.

For Filling: Whip the cream with the pudding mix until stiff peaks form. The pudding mix stabilizes the whipped cream and keeps it from separating.

> "I attribute many cures of chronic dyspepsia to the regular use of chocolate."
> – Dr. Francois Joseph Victor Broussais (1772-1838), France

For Assembly: Place a cake layer on a serving plate. Spread half of the whipped cream on the layer and dot with fresh berries. Top with a second cake layer. Spread with remaining whipped cream and dot with remaining berries. Top with third cake layer. Frost sides and top with buttercream.

Broken Top Restaurant, Bend, Oregon

Chocolate Mousse Cake

Chocolate Mousse Cake, Broken Top Restaurant's signature dessert, is an impressive five inches of soft cake with a light chocolate flavor, followed by a thick layer of intensely chocolate mousse, and topped with a creamy smooth ganache.

Makes 1 10-inch cake

Cake:

6 tablespoons vegetable shortening

3/4 cup plus 2 tablespoons granulated sugar

2 extra-large eggs

1 1/2 cups cake flour

7 tablespoons unsweetened cocoa powder

1 1/2 teaspoons baking powder

1/4 teaspoon baking soda

Pinch salt

1/2 cup milk

1 1/2 tablespoons light corn syrup

1 teaspoon vanilla

Mousse:

18 ounces chopped bittersweet chocolate

2 1/4 cups whipping cream, divided

4 large egg whites

Ganache:

10 ounces chopped bittersweet chocolate

1 1/4 cups whipping cream

For Cake: Preheat oven to 350 degrees. Butter a 10-inch cake pan or springform pan. Line the bottom of the buttered pan with parchment paper.

In a mixer bowl, cream the shortening with the sugar until light and fluffy. Add the eggs, one at a time, beating well after each addition.

In a small bowl, stir together the flour, cocoa, baking powder, baking soda, and salt.

In another small bowl, stir together the milk, corn syrup, and vanilla.

More than 1,200 different compounds make chocolate one of the most complex foods in the world.

Add the flour and milk mixtures alternately to the shortening mixture, beginning and ending with flour. Stir until well combined, about 2 minutes.

Pour into prepared pan and bake for 20 minutes or until top springs back when lightly touched in the center.

Remove from oven and cool on a wire rack to room temperature. Remove from pan and wrap with plastic wrap and freeze.

For Mousse: In the top of a double boiler, melt the chocolate with 1 cup whipping cream, over hot, not boiling, water. Stir to combine. Cool to room temperature, stirring occasionally to facilitate cooling.

When chocolate is cool, whip the remaining 1 1/4 cups whipping cream to medium peaks. Set aside.

In a clean bowl, whip the egg whites until stiff peaks form. Set aside.

Carefully fold the whipped cream into the chocolate in thirds. Add the egg whites and gently fold into the chocolate mixture until well combined. Set aside in refrigerator.

For Ganache: In the top of a double boiler, melt the chocolate with the cream. Stir frequently until just combined. Remove from heat and cool to room temperature, stirring frequently while cooling.

To Assemble: Remove cake from freezer and cut dome off of top so cake is level.

Place a 4-inch tall parchment paper collar around the cake so that it is 2 inches above the top of the cake. Secure with tape and reinforce by placing a 10-inch springform ring around the outside of the cake.

Pour the mousse into the collar, spreading from the inside of the top to the outside until the mousse is level. Fill to about 2 inches above the top of the cake. Refrigerate (do not freeze) and let set overnight.

Remove cake from refrigerator and carefully remove springform ring and paper collar. Trim any ragged edges of the mousse with a sharp, hot, wet knife.

Place the cake on a wire rack over a rimmed baking sheet to catch ganache drips.

Place the ganache in a spouted vessel (such as a spouted glass measuring cup or gravy boat). Pour the ganache in a circular motion from the inside of the cake to the edges, being sure to completely cover the top and sides of the cake.

Refrigerate to set the ganache, about 20 minutes. When ready to serve, cut with a hot, damp knife.

Note: See raw egg caution, page 18.

The Berlin Inn, Portland, Oregon
Apricot Cappuccino Torte

The Berlin Inn's Apricot Cappuccino Cake features alternating layers of delicate chocolate sponge cake, light-as-air espresso chantilly cream, and imported apricot preserves. It's a unique and delightful combination.

Makes 1 9-inch torte

Sponge Cake:
- 4 egg yolks, room temperature
- 2 tablespoons warm water
- 1/2 cup granulated sugar, divided
- 1/2 teaspoon vanilla
- 1/4 teaspoon almond extract
- Pinch cinnamon
- 3 egg whites
- 1/2 cup plus 1 tablespoon all-purpose flour
- 1 tablespoon unsweetened cocoa powder
- 3 tablespoons cornstarch
- 1/2 teaspoon baking powder

Whipped Cream Filling:
- 2 cups whipping cream
- 1 teaspoon vanilla
- 2 tablespoons powdered sugar
- 1 1/2 tablespoons instant coffee powder

Assembly:
- 3/4 cup apricot brandy
- 2 cups apricot jam
- 12 chocolate covered coffee beans
- Shaved chocolate for garnish

For Sponge Cake: Preheat oven to 350 degrees. Grease a 9-inch cake pan.

In a large bowl with an electric mixer, whip the egg yolks with the water until frothy. Add 6 tablespoons sugar, a little at a time, whipping until the mixture is thick and creamy. Add the vanilla, almond extract, and cinnamon, blend well.

In a separate bowl, with clean beaters, whip the egg whites until stiff but not dry.

Pour the whites over the yolk mixture and then sift the flour, cocoa, cornstarch, and baking powder over the whites. Gently fold the dry ingredients and egg whites into the yolk mixture.

Spread the batter in the prepared pan and bake for 30 to 35 minutes or until the center springs back when touched.

Remove from oven and cool for 10 minutes. Remove from pan and cool completely on wire rack.

For Whipped Filling: Combine the cream, powdered sugar, vanilla, and coffee powder in a chilled bowl. Whip until stiff peaks form.

For Assembly: Slice the sponge cake into three layers. Brush all of the layers with apricot brandy.

Place one layer on a serving plate. Using a pastry bag with a plain tip, pipe three spirals of whipped filling onto the cake layer. Using another pastry bag, spiral the apricot jam between the whipped filling spirals. Top with a second layer of cake.

Top the second layer with 3/4 cup whipped filling. Spread filling evenly. Place the last layer of cake on top. Skim coat the top and sides with whipped filling.

Using a pastry bag with a #5 tip, make a lattice pattern on the top of the cake. Drizzle some apricot jam over the lattice using a #43 tip. Mark each serving with a coffee bean. Garnish sides with shaved chocolate.

Recipe Tester's note: If you don't have a pastry bag, place ingredients to be piped into a plastic sandwich bag and snip off the end of one corner. For a larger pastry tip, cut a bigger hole in the bag.

Oxidation and other chemical interactions make fine dark chocolate, like red wine, improve with age. Because of the milk proteins, milk chocolate is best if used within a few months.

Triple Chocolate Cake with Mulled Cabernet Sauvignon Sauce

Pastry chef Randall Hatfield's Triple Chocolate Cake with Mulled Cabernet Sauvignon Sauce is one of this author's favorite desserts. Each cake is baked in a small tartlet pan, then inverted and served warm in a pool of delectable wine sauce. It's warm, rich, and gooey.

Makes 9 servings

Milk Chocolate Ganache:

10 ounces chopped milk chocolate

1/2 cup whipping cream

Grand Marnier to taste, optional

Chocolate Cake:

3/4 cup granulated sugar

3/4 cup water

1/4 cup cornstarch

9 ounces chopped bittersweet chocolate

1/2 cup plus 2 tablespoons whipping cream

3 lightly beaten eggs, room temperature

White Chocolate Glaze:

7 tablespoons whipping cream

5 ounces chopped white chocolate

1 tablespoon butter, room temperature

2 tablespoons corn syrup

Mulled Cabernet Sauvignon Sauce:

1 bottle (750 ml) inexpensive Cabernet Sauvignon

3 1/2 tablespoons granulated sugar

1/2 vanilla bean

1 whole star anise

1 cinnamon stick

1 slice fresh ginger

For Milk Chocolate Ganache: In a small saucepan, heat the cream until tiny bubbles form around the edges of the pan. Pour the hot cream over the milk chocolate and let stand for one minute. Stir until the chocolate is completely melted and smooth. Add Grand Marnier, if desired. Refrigerate until chilled. When chilled, scoop into 9 small balls. Set aside.

For Chocolate Cake: Combine the sugar and water in a small saucepan and bring to a boil. Remove from heat and allow to cool. When almost cool, stir in cornstarch until smooth. Set aside.

In the top of a double boiler, melt the chocolate over hot water. When chocolate is completely melted, add the cream and stir until well combined.

Add the beaten eggs to the chocolate mixture and whisk until combined. Add the cornstarch mixture and whisk until batter is smooth.

For White Chocolate Glaze: In a small saucepan, heat the cream until tiny bubbles form around the edges of the pan. Pour the hot cream over the white chocolate and let stand for one minute. Stir until the chocolate is completely melted and smooth. Whisk in the butter and corn syrup. Let cool at room temperature. Heat in microwave for about 15 seconds to warm for serving.

For Mulled Cabernet Sauvignon Sauce: Combine the wine and sugar in a heavy bottomed flameproof casserole or saucepan.

Tie the vanilla bean, star anise, cinnamon stick, and ginger slice in a piece of cheesecloth. Add to the wine mixture.

Over a very low flame, reduce wine by two thirds (2/3) to a thick, syrupy consistency that coats a spoon easily. Keep the wine to just below a simmer, taking many hours to reduce. Allow to cool. Remove cheesecloth bag.

Assembly and Baking: Spray 9 4-inch molds (brioche molds work well) with non-stick spray or brush with melted butter.

Fill the molds 2/3 full with batter. Place a milk chocolate ganache ball in the center of each mold. Finish filling each mold, covering ganache with batter.

Freeze the unbaked cakes overnight. By freezing you will ensure that the cake will bake well before the ganache starts to melt.

Preheat oven to 325 degrees.

Place frozen cakes directly into preheated oven. Bake for about 15 minutes, until the cakes have set. Turn oven off and let rest, with the door ajar, for another 15 minutes. Unmold.

Serve cake warm, sitting in a pool of Mulled Cabernet Sauvignon Sauce with White Chocolate Glaze on top of the cake. It goes great with Vanilla Bean Ice Cream!

Chef's note: Baking these cakes is tricky due to the ganache center. The top of the cake may fall slightly while cooling. Invert to show off the smooth bottom of the cake.

It is also possible to bake the cakes immediately after filling the molds. However, the freezing method enhances the baking procedure.

Recipe Tester's note: The wine sauce, the ganache, and the chocolate glaze can be made a day or two ahead.

Café des Amis, Portland, Oregon

Black Walnut-Banana Cake with Chocolate Rum Frosting

Pastry chef Steve Smith's dessert isn't long on chocolate, but the moist cake is packed with banana flavor and the Chocolate Rum Frosting makes a great contrast. Our recipe tester reports that this cake is a great one for licking the bowl while making!

Makes 1 9-inch cake

Black Walnut-Banana Cake:
6 tablespoons butter

3/4 cup granulated sugar

4 eggs, separated

1/2 teaspoon salt

1 tablespoon vanilla

1 tablespoon banana liqueur, optional

1 1/2 mashed ripe bananas

2/3 cup black walnuts

2/3 cup all-purpose flour

1 teaspoon baking powder

Chocolate Rum Frosting:
8 ounces chopped bittersweet chocolate

1/2 cup butter

1/4 cup corn syrup

3/4 cup whipping cream

1 tablespoon rum

For Black Walnut-Banana Cake: Preheat oven to 350 degrees. Butter and flour a 9 by 2 1/2-inch round pan. Or line the pan with parchment paper. Butter and flour the parchment paper, shaking out any excess flour.

In a large bowl, cream the butter and sugar. Add the egg yolks, one at a time, beating well after each addition. Beat in the salt, vanilla, banana liqueur if desired, and mashed bananas.

Combine the walnuts, flour, and baking powder in the bowl of a food processor. Process until the walnuts are finely ground. Fold the flour mixture into the banana mixture.

In a large bowl, whip the egg whites until stiff peaks form. Fold the egg whites into the banana mixture.

Pour the batter into the prepared pan. Bake for 40 to 45 minutes or until a toothpick inserted in the center of the cake comes out clean. Cool for 10 minutes. Turn out of pan and cool completely on wire rack. Slice cooled cake into three layers.

For Chocolate Rum Frosting: In the top of a double boiler, melt the chocolate and butter over hot water. Stir until smooth.

Transfer melted chocolate to the bowl of an electric mixer and add the corn syrup, whipping cream and rum. Beat, at high speed, until light and smooth. Use to fill and frost the Black Walnut-Banana Cake.

Caffeine and theobromine, both central nervous system stimulants, make chocolate an excellent energy-booster.

Caprial's Bistro, Portland, Oregon
Chocolate Turtle Torte

Restaurant owner and television chef, Caprial Spence, charms her audiences with her Public Television show, "Cooking with Caprial." Her Chocolate Turtle Torte, which combines three of this author's favorite flavors–chocolate, pecans, and caramel–will charm you too. This no-bake dessert is rich and custard-like with a crunchy crust that's accented with a hint of cinnamon.

Makes 1 10-inch torte

Pastry:
1 3/4 cup cake flour

2 tablespoons granulated sugar

1/2 cup chilled butter

1 egg

1 to 2 tablespoons water

Praline Filling:
1 1/2 cup granulated sugar

1/2 cup water

3/4 cup plus 2 tablespoons butter

3/4 cup milk

1/3 cup honey

3 cups pecan pieces

Mousse:
6 egg yolks

1 cup powdered sugar

1/4 cup liqueur (brandy, orange brandy, or dark rum)

6 egg whites

Pinch cream of tartar

1 pound chopped bittersweet chocolate

1/2 cup butter

2 cups whipping cream

Ganache Topping:
8 ounces chopped semi-sweet chocolate

3/4 cup whipping cream

For Pastry: Combine the flour and sugar in a bowl. Cut in butter until the mixture resembles coarse meal. Add the egg and 1 tablespoon water and mix and toss until combined. Add an additional tablespoon water if mixture is too dry to hold together.

On a lightly floured surface, roll out dough to a 12-inch round. Fit into a 10-inch springform pan. Set aside.

For Praline Filling: Combine sugar and water in a heavy bottomed saucepan. Heat over medium heat until sugar turns a light amber color, about 15 to 20 minutes. Cover the pan for the first 30 seconds or until any sugar crystals on the sides of the pan have dissolved, or wash sugar crystals off of the sides of the pan with a pastry brush dipped in water. Once the sugar mixture starts to boil do not stir.

When the sugar has reached a light amber color, add the butter and milk and let simmer for 15 minutes. Stir in honey and nuts. Cool.

While praline is cooling, preheat oven to 350 degrees.

Pour praline mixture into crust, folding the sides of the crust in loosely. Bake for 20 to 25 minutes or until crust is golden brown. Cool completely.

> Try dusting a greased chocolate cake pan with cocoa instead of flour. It looks and tastes great!

For Mousse: In the top of a double boiler, combine the egg yolks, sugar, and liqueur. Cook over simmering water while whisking, until the mixture has thickened into a light foamy custard.

In the top of another double boiler, melt the chocolate and butter over hot water. Stir until smooth. Cool slightly.

Fold the cooled chocolate into the egg yolk mixture.

In a large bowl, whip the egg whites until medium peaks form. In a separate bowl, whip the cream. Fold the egg whites and whipped cream into the chocolate mixture. Chill.

When mousse is chilled, spread over the praline.

For Ganache Topping: In the top of a double boiler, melt the chocolate with the cream, stirring until smooth. Cool.

Pour cooled ganache topping over mousse and refrigerate. Serve chilled.

Recipe Tester's note: For best results, this torte should be chilled for several hours or overnight. Don't worry if the caramel tends to "weep" a bit once the torte has been sliced.

Caprial's Chocolate Silk

Many chefs make chocolate silk. This no-bake dessert, developed by chef Mark Dowers and served at Caprial's Bistro, is especially memorable with a rich, custard-like texture and a crisp, cinnamon-flavored crust.

Makes 1 9-inch pie (8 to 12 servings)

Crust:

1 cup pecans

1 1/2 cups chocolate cookie crumbs (made from Nabisco Famous Chocolate Wafers™)

1 cup firmly packed brown sugar

1/4 teaspoon cinnamon

1/8 teaspoon nutmeg

1 cup melted unsalted butter

Filling:

1 pound chopped bittersweet chocolate

1/2 cup unsalted butter, softened

1 cup granulated sugar

7 eggs, room temperature

1/4 cup brandy

1 teaspoon vanilla

1/4 cup half and half

Whipped cream for garnish

For Crust: Combine the pecans, cookie crumbs, brown sugar, cinnamon, and nutmeg in the bowl of a food processor. Process for about 5 seconds and then add the butter. Once the butter is incorporated, process until the crust holds together when pressed with finger tips, about 30 to 45 seconds. Press the crust into a 9-inch springform pan. Chill for 30 minutes.

For Filling: In the top of a double boiler, melt the chocolate over hot water until the chocolate reaches 150 degrees.

While the chocolate is melting, combine the butter and sugar in a mixer bowl. Using the whip attachment, whip until the mixture is fluffy, about 2 minutes,

Before the Industrial Revolution, chocolate was so expensive it could only be enjoyed by the rich. The invention of the cocoa press and the mass production of chocolate finally brought chocolate within reach of ordinary citizens.

stopping to scrape down the sides of the bowl several times. Add the eggs, one at a time, beating well after each addition. The mixture may look separated, that is normal.

With the mixer running at low to medium speed, add the hot melted chocolate, stopping to scrape down the sides often.

Add the brandy, vanilla, and half and half. Continue to whip for about 2 minutes or until the mixture is silky and shiny. Make sure to scrape down the sides one last time and then pour into the prepared crust. Chill for at least 2 to 4 hours before serving. Serve with whipped cream.

Recipe Tester's note: The key to success with this recipe is to beat the filling until it's really light and fluffy.

Note: See raw egg caution, page 18.

Gerry's Chocolate Cake

Throughout Oregon, Gerry Frank is affectionately known as "Mr. Chocolate." In Salem, Gerry Frank's Konditorei is "chocolate cake central." The buttercream on Gerry's Chocolate Cake is so light it's almost fluffy.

Makes 1 9-inch cake

Cake:

- 2 1/2 cups all-purpose flour
- 1 1/2 teaspoons baking soda
- 1 teaspoon baking powder
- 1/2 cup unsweetened cocoa powder
- 1/2 teaspoon salt
- 2/3 cup butter
- 1 3/4 cups granulated sugar
- 2 eggs
- 1/2 cup water
- 1 teaspoon vanilla
- 1 cup buttermilk

Frosting:

- 1 6-ounce package chocolate chips
- 1/2 cup half and half
- 1 cup butter
- 2 1/2 cups powdered sugar

For Cake: Preheat oven to 350 degrees. Butter and flour two 9-inch cake pans. Line the bottom of each pan with waxed or parchment paper, then butter and flour the paper.

Sift together the flour, baking soda, baking powder, cocoa, and salt. Set aside.

In the bowl of an electric mixer, cream the butter. Gradually add the sugar and beat at medium speed for 1 minute. Add the eggs, one at a time, beating 1 minute after each addition. Gradually add the water and vanilla and beat for 1 minute. Do not overbeat.

With the mixer on low speed, alternately add the flour mixture and the buttermilk. Add the flour in four parts and the buttermilk in three parts, beginning and ending with flour. Blend only until the flour no longer shows. Do not overbeat.

Some cultures toast happiness with champagne. Many Mexicans celebrate with hot, sweetened cocoa.

Pour the batter into the prepared pans and tap once to settle the batter. Bake for 25-30 minutes, or until a toothpick inserted in the center of the cake comes out clean. Cool the cake for 10 minutes in the pans before inverting onto wire racks. Cool completely before frosting.

For Frosting: Combine the chocolate chips, butter, and half and half in a saucepan. Melt over medium heat, stirring constantly until the mixture is smooth. Whisk in the powdered sugar. In a bowl, set over ice, beat the frosting with a wire whisk (or electric beater) until the frosting holds its shape, about 20 minutes. Fill and frost the cooled cake layers.

Chocolate Hazelnut Torte with Crème Anglaise

This wonderful recipe, created by executive chef Bill Reicheback, caused us to shout, "Stop the presses!" We discovered it at a Chocolate Lover's Weekend at the Geiser Grand Hotel in Baker City and just had to include it.

Makes 1 9-inch torte

Filling:
1/2 cup granulated sugar

1/4 cup water

1/4 cup Frangelico (hazelnut liqueur)

1 cup butter (2 sticks)

1 cup cream

1/4 cup honey

2 1/2 cups toasted hazelnuts, skinned and chopped

Cake:
1 1/2 cups toasted hazelnuts, skinned

1 cup sugar

6 ounces bittersweet chocolate

6 ounces semi-sweet chocolate

2 ounces white chocolate

3/4 cup unsalted butter, room temperature

8 eggs, separated

2 teaspoons vanilla

1/2 cup all-purpose flour

1/2 teaspoon salt

1/2 teaspoon cream of tartar

Dark Chocolate Ganache Topping:
8 ounces bittersweet chocolate, chopped

8 ounces semi-sweet chocolate, chopped

4 ounces white chocolate, chopped

2 1/2 cups cream

Crème Anglaise:
1 1/4 cups cream

1 teaspoon vanilla

3 egg yolks

2 tablespoons sugar

1/4 cup Frangelico or amaretto (optional)

For Filling: In a small, heavy bottomed saucepan, combine sugar, water, and Frangelico. Heat over medium-high heat until the mixture turns a light amber color. Add butter and cream and simmer for 15 minutes. Take off the heat and stir in honey and the chopped hazelnuts. Allow to cool completely.

For the Cake: Preheat oven to 375 degrees. Butter the sides and bottom of two 9-inch springform pans and line the bottoms with parchment or waxed paper.

In the bowl of a food processor, chop the hazelnuts finely with 4 tablespoons of sugar. Set aside.

In the top of a double boiler, melt the chocolates with the softened butter. Stir until smooth.

In a bowl, whisk egg yolks with 2/3 cup sugar. Stir in chocolate mixture and vanilla.

Mix the flour and salt with the hazelnuts and fold into the chocolate mixture.

In a large bowl, beat the egg whites with cream of tarter until soft peaks form. Add the remaining sugar and beat until the whites are stiff but not dry. Fold a spoonful of the egg whites into the chocolate mixture (to lighten it). Then carefully fold in the remaining egg white mixture. Divide the batter into 2 prepared pans. Bake for 30-35 minutes. Cool completely on wire racks.

For the Dark Ganache: In a saucepan, heat cream until bubbles begin to form around the edges. Place the chopped chocolate in a bowl and pour the hot cream over the chocolate. Let sit for 5 minutes. Stir to ensure the chocolate is melted and smooth. Allow to cool to room temperature.

Assembly: After the cakes are cool, set them on a table and trim the tops so they are flat. Spread the hazelnut filling on the top of the bottom cake. Place the second cake on top of the filling and press gently.

Place the cake on a wire rack with a baking pan or cookie sheet under to catch the excess ganache. Pour the dark chocolate ganache over the top of the cake slowly covering all of the cake. (The ganache should be pourable. Re-warm slightly, if needed.) Use a rubber spatula to guide the ganache into any openings on the sides of the cake. Decorate with chocolate curls and whole hazelnuts. Chill on wire racks for 4 hours until firm. Run a knife under the cake to remove to a platter. Serve with crème anglaise.

For Crème Anglaise: In a small saucepan, heat cream until bubbles form around the sides of the pan.

In a bowl, beat together egg yolks and sugar. Very slowly pour cream into egg mixture. Add liqueur. Return the mixture to the saucepan and heat until hot, but not boiling. Cook until thick. Strain out any bits of cooked egg. Cool. Spoon a generous amount of the sauce onto each plate. Place a serving of the torte in the center and enjoy.

Recipe Tester's note: The ganache should be liquid enough to pour, but not so warm that it runs off the cake. If too much ganache runs off, let the ganache cool. Then re-pour the excess ganache from the catch pan onto the cake. Left-over ganache can be use as ice cream topping.

Soufflé

It's not quite a cake.
It's not exactly a pudding.
A chocolate soufflé is a
feather-light bit of heaven.

The Place Next to the San Juan Ferry, Friday Harbor, Washington

Chocolate Grand Marnier Truffle Soufflé

This soufflé is a little different because a truffle is placed in the middle before baking. The truffle's dark chocolate and Grand Mariner give a veritable explosion of flavor in the center of the dessert.

Makes 8 servings

Truffles:
6 tablespoons whipping cream
5 ounces chopped bittersweet or semi-sweet chocolate (use high-quality chocolate such as Lindt or Callebaut)
1 tablespoon Grand Marnier

Chocolate Soufflé:
9 tablespoons granulated sugar, divided
2 tablespoons cornstarch
1 1/2 tablespoons cocoa powder
1 cup whole milk
1 1/2 tablespoons butter
6 ounces chopped bittersweet or semi-sweet chocolate
2 teaspoons vanilla extract
3 tablespoons Grand Marnier
6 eggs, separated, divided
Powdered sugar for garnish
Whipped Cream for garnish

For Truffles: In a small saucepan, bring the cream to a boil. Add chocolate and remove from heat. Let stand for a few minutes and then whisk until the chocolate is melted and the mixture is smooth. Add Grand Marnier and mix well. Refrigerate until chilled and set, about 40 minutes.

Place plastic wrap on a cold plate. With a tablespoon, spoon little balls of the chocolate mixture and place on plate. You should get about 8 portions. Working quickly, roll each portion into a ball with your hands. Dust hands with cocoa powder if chocolate gets too soft to handle. Freeze the truffles for at least 1 hour, then cover completely if not to be used right away. These can be kept frozen for several weeks.

For Chocolate Soufflé: Preheat oven to 500 degrees. Butter 8 6-ounce soufflé cups and sprinkle with granulated sugar.

In a mixing bowl or the top of a double boiler, stir together 6 tablespoons sugar, cornstarch, and cocoa powder. Make sure there are no lumps. Stir in the milk. Place over a pan of boiling water and add butter, chopped chocolate, vanilla, and Grand Marnier. Whisk for a few minutes until smooth.

Beat the egg yolks in a separate bowl. Slowly add the hot milk mixture to yolks, whipping constantly until well blended. Place back over boiling water and whisk until very thick, like custard. Remove from heat and cool until just warm.

Whip egg whites until soft peaks form. Gradually add 3 tablespoons sugar and continue beating until stiff peaks form. The whites should be glossy but not dry. Fold the whites into the warm chocolate mixture 1/2 at a time. Fold carefully to insure that the mixture retains its lightness.

Place one truffle in each prepared cup and then fill almost to the top with the chocolate mixture. Turn oven down to 400 degrees and place soufflés on baking sheets. Bake for 12 to 15 minutes. The tops will rise and form a small indentation in the center of each soufflé. When the indentations are gone the soufflés are done.

Dust with powdered sugar and serve with a dollop of whipped cream on the side.

> Chocolate is velvety on the tongue thanks to Swiss chocolatier Rondolphe Lindt. In 1879, he invented "conching," heating, rolling, and blending chocolate for a smooth mouthfeel.

Chocolate Soufflé Tartlets

At your next dinner party, impress your friends with these individual soufflés by chef Lydia Bugatti. They have an intense semi-sweet dark chocolate flavor for serious chocolate fans.

Makes 7-8 tartlets

Tartlets:
1/2 cup milk

1 1/4 cups granulated sugar, divided

7 ounces chopped unsweetened chocolate

6 egg whites

Pinch cream of tartar

4 egg yolks

Warm Chocolate Sauce:
4 ounces chopped semi-sweet chocolate

1/2 cup whipping cream

Whipped Cream:
1 cup whipping cream

1 teaspoon granulated sugar

For Tartlets: Preheat oven to 400 degrees. Place a sheet of parchment on a baking sheet. Arrange 7 or 8 4- by 1 1/2-inch tartlet tins without bottoms on the parchment. Spray with non-stick spray.

Bring milk and 1 cup sugar to a boil, add chocolate, and stir to melt. Let chocolate mixture cool for 10 minutes.

In a mixing bowl, whisk egg whites with cream of tartar until soft peaks form. Slowly add 1/4 cup sugar and whisk until stiff.

Stir egg yolks into cooled chocolate mixture and quickly fold in egg whites in thirds.

Divide batter among prepared tins, filling to within 1/4-inch of the tops. Use extra tins if needed.

Bake for 15 minutes or until tops are cracking. If you smell chocolate, start checking but don't open the oven door before the final few minutes or the tartlets won't rise properly.

Cocoa and baking chocolate contain no cholesterol. Milk chocolate, because of its milk content, contains a small amount of cholesterol.

Remove from oven and, as the tartlets cool, help them back into the tins by gently pushing the sides in and allowing them to settle. When cool, wrap and refrigerate until needed. They will keep for 4 days.

For Chocolate Sauce: Combine the chocolate and cream in a small microwave-safe bowl. Microwave on low power, stirring occasionally, until the chocolate is melted and the sauce is smooth.

For Whipped Cream: Combine cream and sugar in a chilled bowl and beat with chilled beaters until soft peaks form.

To Serve: Sprinkle a plate with powdered sugar. Place a tartlet in the center of the plate. Microwave for 20 seconds to warm. Drizzle with 2 tablespoons Warm Chocolate Sauce. Top with barely sweetened whipped cream. Repeat with remaining tartlets.

Chocolate Soufflé

If you're in Vancouver, British Columbia at the Wedgewood Hotel's Bacchus Ristorante, this excellent chocolate soufflé is worth the 20 minute wait. Or you can thrill your family or special guests by making it at home.

Makes 6 servings

> 6 ounces chopped semi-sweet chocolate
> 1/4 cup plus 1/3 cup granulated sugar, divided
> 7 eggs, separated
> 1 ounce Grand Marnier
> Powdered sugar for garnish

Preheat oven to 400 degrees. Place a large pan half filled with hot water in the oven. Lightly butter and sugar 6 6-ounce soufflé cups or custard cups.

In the top of a double boiler, melt the chocolate over hot water. Whisk in the egg yolks, 1/4 cup sugar, and the liqueur.

In a large mixer bowl with wire whip attachment, whip the egg whites. Gradually add the 1/3 cup sugar. Continue whipping until soft peaks form. Gently fold the egg whites into the chocolate mixture.

Pour batter into prepared soufflé cups and place in the hot water bath. Bake for 20-30 minutes or until puffed and dry on top. Dust with powdered sugar and serve immediately.

> Tumbadores who harvest cacao pods, which contain the cacoa beans from which chocolate is made, use machetes to split up to 500 pods an hour.

"If this is heaven, where's the chocolate?"

— bronze crypt plaque in a Los Angeles cemetary

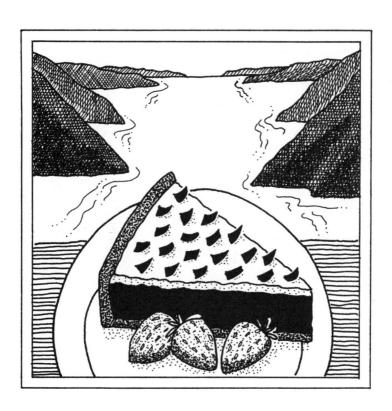

Cheesecakes

There's something wonderful
about the cheesy richness
of a good cheesecake.
Add chocolate and you've
got something really special.

The Belmont, Port Townsend, Washington

Chambord Chocolate Cheesecake

At The Belmont in Port Townsend, Washington, they serve this excellent cheesecake made by Uptown Custom Catering. This is a velvety smooth cheesecake with just the right cheese/chocolate combination.

Makes 1 10-inch cheesecake

Crust:

1 9-ounce package chocolate wafer cookies **
6 tablespoons unsalted butter, melted
2 teaspoons granulated sugar

Filling:

3 8-ounce packages cream cheese
1/2 cup granulated sugar
6 ounces Belgian chocolate, melted (preferably Callebaut)
1/2 cup Chambord liqueur (black raspberry liqueur)
4 eggs
1/2 cup whipping cream

Topping:

2 cups sour cream
1/2 cup granulated sugar
1 cup whipping cream
Fresh mint sprigs for garnish

** Nabisco Famous Chocolate Wafers™ work well.

For Crust: Position rack in the center of the oven and preheat to 350 degrees. Butter a 10-inch springform pan. Chill and set aside.

Place the chocolate wafers in the bowl of a food processor and process until finely ground. Add the butter and sugar and process until moist crumbs form. Press into the bottom and sides of the prepared springform pan.

For Filling: Using an electric mixer with paddle, beat the cream cheese until completely smooth. Add the sugar and beat three minutes. Add melted chocolate and blend well. Stir in Chambord until well combined.

With the mixer set at medium sped, add the eggs one at a time, beating well after each addition. Scrape down the sides of the bowl after each egg is beaten into the filling. Do not over beat the eggs as this may cause the top of the cheesecake to crack. Add the cream and stir to blend well.

Pour the filling into the crust-lined pan. Bake for 60-70 minutes or until the filling is almost set. The center should still move slightly. Transfer to a rack and cool to room temperature. Chill overnight.

For Topping: Preheat the oven to 400 degrees. Combine the sour cream and sugar until smooth. Spoon 2/3 of the sour cream mixture over the top of the cheesecake, leaving a 2-inch border. Bake 10 minutes or until the topping is set and slightly golden. Chill again.

When cold and firm, spoon the remaining sour cream mixture into the center of the cheesecake. Chill.

In a medium bowl, whip the whipping cream until firm peaks form. Transfer the whipped cream to a pastry bag with a medium star tip. Pipe whipped cream stars around the 2-inch border on top of the cheesecake. Garnish with fresh mint sprigs.

Spain kept how to manufacture chocolate a secret for more than 100 years. However, in 1606, Italian traveler Antonio Carletti uncovered the secret and brought chocolate processing to other parts of Europe.

Recipe Tester's note: For this and other cheesecake recipes, it's a good idea to bring the cream cheese to room temperature before mixing to ensure a smooth texture.

Visconti's, Wenatchee, Washington

White Chocolate Truffle Cheesecake with Raspberry Sauce

With their authentic sauces and perfect al dente pasta, Visconti's is a must-stop whenever this author is in Wenatchee, Washington. You can top your meal off with chef Daniel Carr's wonderful White Chocolate Truffle Cheesecake.

Makes 1 10-inch cheesecake

Crust:
- 1/2 cup almonds
- 4 tablespoons unsalted butter, melted
- 1 cup graham cracker crumbs
- 1/2 teaspoon ground cinnamon

Raspberry Melba:
- 2 tablespoons red currant jelly
- 1/4 cup raspberry purée
- 1/4 teaspoon cornstarch
- Pinch salt
- 2 tablespoons granulated sugar

Filling:
- 4 8-ounce packages cream cheese
- 1 1/4 cups granulated sugar
- 4 eggs
- 1 cup Ghirardelli Ground White Chocolate
- 1/4 cup whipping cream
- 1/4 cup sour cream

For Crust: Preheat oven to 350 degrees. Double wrap the bottom plate of a 10-inch springform pan with aluminum foil and then attach the bottom of the springform pan to the sides.

In the bowl of a food processor, grind the almonds until they are a fine powder. Add the melted butter, graham cracker crumbs, and cinnamon and pulse 2 or 3 times to combine. Press the graham cracker mixture firmly onto the bottom of the prepared pan. Bake for 10 minutes. Remove from oven and cool.

According to the American Dental Association, chocolate helps prevent cavities. Chemicals in chocolate neutralize the decay-producing effects of sugar.

For Raspberry Melba: Combine the jelly, raspberry purée, cornstarch, salt, and sugar in a small saucepan. Stir until smooth, making sure the cornstarch is well combined. Cook over low heat, stirring constantly, until thick and clear. Cool.

For Filling: In a large mixer bowl, beat the cream cheese until smooth. Gradually add the sugar and continue beating until well combined. Add the eggs, one at a time, beating well after each addition. Add ground white chocolate, whipping cream, and sour cream and mix until smooth.

Lightly butter the sides of the cooled springform pan. Pour in the cream cheese filling. Carefully pour the Raspberry Melba onto the filling making a pattern or design of your choice. Or use a knife to swirl the Raspberry Melba.

Set the pan on a large piece of aluminum foil. Wrap the bottom and sides of the pan to insure the pan is waterproof. Do not let foil go over the top edge of the pan.

Place the wrapped pan into a larger pan and pour boiling water into the larger pan until the water comes about 2/3 of the way up the sides of the springform pan. Bake for 1 1/2 hours. The cheesecake is done when a toothpick inserted in the center of the pan comes out perfectly clean.

Remove from oven and cool on a wire rack to room temperature. Refrigerate cooled cheesecake for 8 hours to set. Do not refrigerate the cheesecake while still warm or the cake may sweat.

Mocha Cheesecake

Lynn Berman's Mocha Cheesecake features a buttery almond crust. The filling has a creamy texture with a deep mocha-chocolate flavor.

Makes 1 10-inch cheesecake

Almond Crust:

1 cup toasted whole almonds (see note)

2 tablespoons granulated sugar

2 tablespoons all-purpose flour

2 tablespoons butter

1/4 cup bittersweet chocolate, finely ground in a food processor

Filling:

6 eggs

1 cup granulated sugar

5 8-ounce packages cream cheese

1/2 cup brewed espresso coffee

3 ounces bittersweet chocolate, melted

For Crust: Preheat oven to 350 degrees.

Place toasted almonds, sugar, and flour in the bowl of a food processor and process until the almonds are a fine powder. Add the butter and pulse two or three times until well incorporated.

Pat the almond mixture onto the bottom and slightly up the sides of a 10-inch springform pan. Bake for 12 minutes. Remove from oven and sprinkle ground chocolate evenly over the hot crust. Set aside.

For Topping: Place the eggs in the bowl of a food processor and process until well beaten. Add sugar and process 15 seconds. With the processor running, add the cream cheese a little at a time. Process until smooth, occasionally scraping down the sides of the bowl. Add the espresso in a thin stream, processing until well incorporated.

> The first chocolate house in Europe opened in London in 1675. Chocolate drinks sold for 10-15 shillings per pound.

For a solid mocha cheesecake, add the chocolate to the cheese mixture in the food processor and process until well blended. Pour into the crust lined pan.

Or, for a marbled mocha cheesecake, pour the cheese filling into the baked almond crust. Drizzle the melted chocolate over the filling and, with a knife, gently swirl the chocolate through the filling.

Cover the bottom and outside of the springform pan with a large sheet of heavy-duty aluminum foil and place in a larger pan. Pour boiling water around the springform pan until the water reaches about halfway up the sides of the pan. Lightly cover the springform pan with foil and bake for 90-105 minutes or until the cake jiggles slightly in the center. (You may need to add more water about halfway through the baking.) Cool on wire rack for 1 hour and then refrigerate until chilled or at least two hours.

Recipe Tester's note: To toast almonds, place on a baking pan in a single layer and bake at 350 degrees for 10 minutes or until golden brown.

La Conner Seafood & Prime Rib House, La Conner, Washington

Chocolate Cheesecake

This creamy cheesecake, a signature dessert at La Conner Seafood and Prime Rib House, is swirled with bittersweet chocolate.

Makes 1 10-inch cheesecake

Crust:

2 1/4 cups graham cracker crumbs
6 tablespoons granulated sugar
1/2 teaspoon ground cinnamon
1/2 cup melted butter

Filling:

4 8-ounce packages cream cheese
1 1/3 cups granulated sugar
5 eggs
1 tablespoon vanilla
1/2 teaspoon almond extract
1 3/4 cups sour cream
2 ounces melted bittersweet chocolate (preferably Callebaut)
2 tablespoons brewed coffee

Preheat oven to 225 degrees. Butter a 10-inch springform pan.

For Crust: In a small bowl, stir together the graham cracker crumbs, sugar, cinnamon, and melted butter until crumbly. Press onto the bottom and up the sides of the prepared springform pan. Set aside.

For Filling: In the bowl of an electric mixer, combine the cream cheese and sugar, beating on medium speed until smooth. Scrape down the sides of the bowl occasionally.

Add the eggs, one at a time, beating well after each addition. Beat in the vanilla and almond extract and then add the sour cream. Beat at low speed until smooth.

> The meat of the cacao bean is used to make chocolate. The cacao shells are ground to make fertilizer. They give gardens a delicious chocolatey smell.

Pour 3/4 of the batter into the prepared crust. Add the melted chocolate and coffee to the remaining 1/4 batter. Mix well. Drop the chocolate batter in spoonfuls on top of the cheesecake. Swirl the chocolate into the cheesecake batter.

Bake for 2 hours or until set. Cool on wire rack. Chill before serving.

Lord Bennett's, Bandon, Oregon

Kahlua Coffee Cheesecake

Espresso lovers will enjoy this cheesecake—it's got a real coffee punch!

Makes 1 10-inch cheesecake

Crust:

1 1/2 cups graham cracker crumbs

1/4 cup granulated sugar

1/4 cup firmly packed brown sugar

1 tablespoon melted butter

Filling:

6 8-ounce packages cream cheese, room temperature

1 1/2 cups granulated sugar

5 eggs, 2 teaspoons vanilla

2/3 cup Kahlua liqueur

1/4 cup hot coffee

1 heaping teaspoon instant coffee crystals

Frosting:

6 ounces semi-sweet chocolate chips, melted

3/4 cup sour cream

Preheat oven to 325 degrees. Butter a 10-inch springform pan.

For Crust: In a small bowl, combine the graham cracker crumbs, white and brown sugars, and melted butter. Stir well. Press onto the bottom of the prepared pan. Set aside.

For Filling: In a large bowl with an electric mixer beat together the cream cheese and sugar until smooth. Add the eggs one at a time, beating well after each addition. Scrape down the sides of the bowl occasionally. Add the vanilla and blend well.

In a small bowl, stir together the Kahlua, coffee, and coffee crystals. Add to the cream cheese mixture and blend well.

Pour the cheesecake mixture into the prepared crust and bake for 1 hour 15 minutes or until set in the center. Cool on a wire rack.

For Frosting: In a small bowl, combine the melted chocolate chips and the sour cream. Blend well. Spread over the top of the cooled cheesecake. Chill for several hours before serving.

Silverwater Cafe, Port Townsend, Washington

Chocolate Espresso Cheesecake

Even if you're not a coffee lover, you'll enjoy David Hero's Chocolate Espresso Cheese-cake. The thin crust is topped with a smooth cheesecake that is a rich blending of chocolate and espresso flavors.

Makes 1 10-inch cheesecake

Crust:

1 1/4 cups all-purpose flour

1/4 cup granulated sugar

1/2 cup butter, softened

1 egg yolk

Filling:

2 1/2 8-ounce packages cream cheese

4 eggs

1 cup granulated sugar

2 tablespoons all-purpose flour

2 tablespoons vanilla

1/4 teaspoon salt

12 ounces semi-sweet chocolate

1/4 cup espresso

1/4 cup hot water

Preheat oven to 350 degrees. Butter a 10-inch springform pan.

For Crust: In a small bowl, combine the flour, sugar, butter, and egg yolk until a soft dough forms. Press half of the dough onto the bottom of the buttered pan. Bake for 10 minutes. Let cool at least 15 minutes.

Press the remaining dough evenly 1-1 1/2 inches up the sides of the pan. Set aside.

For Filling: In a mixer bowl, beat the cream cheese, sugar, flour, and one egg until smooth, scraping the bowl and beaters frequently. Add the remaining eggs, one at a time, beating until smooth. Add vanilla and salt.

In a small saucepan over low heat, melt the chocolate in the espresso and hot water. Stir until smooth. Slowly add to the cream cheese mixture, beating until smooth.

Pour filling into prepared crust. Bake for 40 minutes. Cake will be soft but not liquid in the center when done. Let stand 15 minutes. Refrigerate overnight until well chilled.

Gasperetti's, Yakima, Washington

White Chocolate Cheesecake

Chef Brad Patterson shares his incredibly rich recipe for White Chocolate Cheesecake. **The Chocolate Lover's Guide to the Pacific Northwest** *awarded this cheesecake a Best List Award.*

Makes 1 10-inch cheesecake

> 1 tablespoon butter, softened
> 2-3 tablespoons graham cracker crumbs
> 5 8-ounces packages cream cheese
> 1 1/4 cups granulated sugar
> 8 eggs
> 1 3/4 pints sour cream
> 8 ounces white chocolate

Preheat oven to 300 degrees. Butter 1 10-inch springform pan. Dust bottom and sides of pan with graham cracker crumbs.

Melt white chocolate over double boiler. Set aside to cool slightly.

Mix cream cheese and sugar until well combined. Add eggs one at a time, mixing until well combined.

Add white chocolate to cream cheese mixture and mix until smooth.

Bake in a water bath for 2 hours at 300 degrees. Chill in the refrigerator for 24 hours before cutting and serving.

Recipe Tester's note: Before beginning recipe, allow all ingredients to come to room temperature. Otherwise, when you add the melted white chocolate to cold ingredients, the chocolate will harden and be difficult to incorporate into the cream cheese mixture.

In France, the week between Christmas and New Year's is known as the confectioners' truce ("la treve des confiseurs"). All official business of the state stops during this week and French citizens spend their time indulging in chocolate.

Cookies, Bars, & Brownies

Picnics. Barbecues. Sack lunches.
A drive in the country.
Chocolate cookies are the
ultimate in portable desserts.

Death By Chocolate Cookies

At the Bread and Roses Bakery, these Death by Chocolate Cookies are huge (6 inches across) and long on chocolate flavor.

Makes 2 dozen cookies

>   1 pound butter
>   2 1/2 cups granulated sugar
>   2 eggs
>   1 tablespoon vanilla
>   3 3/4 cups all-purpose flour
>   3/4 cup cocoa powder
>   2 1/2 teaspoons baking powder
>   2 teaspoons salt
>   3 cups semi-sweet chocolate chips, divided
>   1 cup melted white chocolate

Preheat oven to 350 degrees.

In a large bowl, cream the butter. Add the sugar and beat until light and fluffy. Add eggs and vanilla and beat well.

In another bowl, stir together the flour, cocoa, baking powder, and salt. Add to creamed mixture and stir to blend well. Stir in 2 cups chocolate chips.

Drop by tablespoonful onto greased baking sheet. Bake about 15 minutes or until set. Cool on wire rack.

Melt the remaining cup chocolate chips over hot water. Dip 1/2 of each cookie into melted semi-sweet chocolate. Drizzle melted white chocolate over each cookie.

Recipe Tester's note: Dipping the cookies in chocolate is optional. These cookies are rich and decadent even without being dipped!

> When chocolate is featured on a magazine cover, sales of the magazine usually double!

Home Fires Bakery, Leavenworth, Washington

Chocolate Fudgenutter Cookies

Home Fires is one of this author's favorite bakeries. Anything from their ovens–from excellent cookies and Chocolate Mint Truffle Pie (see p.120) to their fresh-baked breads–is delightful. These cookies are sure to please those who love peanut butter and chocolate.

Makes 5 dozen cookies

1/2 cup butter
2/3 cup plus 1 3/4 cups semi-sweet chocolate chips, divided
1 1/4 cups granulated sugar
1 1/4 cups firmly packed brown sugar
1 cup vegetable shortening
2 eggs
1 1/2 teaspoons vanilla
2 1/2 cups all-purpose flour
1 teaspoon salt
1 teaspoon baking soda
1 3/4 cups rolled oats
1 cup peanut butter chips

Preheat oven to 325 degrees.

Melt the butter and 2/3 cup chocolate chips in the top of a double boiler over simmering water. Set aside to cool.

In a large bowl of a mixer, cream the sugars and shortening until fluffy. Add the eggs one at a time, beating well after each addition. Beat in the vanilla. Add the melted chocolate mixture and beat until well combined.

In another bowl, mix together the flour, salt, and baking soda. Add to the creamed mixture alternately with the rolled oats and stir to blend. Stir in the remaining chocolate chips and peanut butter chips. Chill.

Drop by rounded tablespoonful onto ungreased baking sheet. Bake for 15 to 16 minutes. Let cool for several minutes before transferring to cooling rack.

Recipe Tester's note: Put cookie dough back into refrigerator between batches for ease of handling.

Anjou Bakery, Cashmere, Washington

Chocolate Smudges

Originally called Soho Globs, these delightful bittersweet/semi-sweet chocolate cookies come from a recipe given to Anjou Bakery by Judy Rosenberg of the Soho Charcuterie in New York. Every Saturday, Anjou Bakery's Heather Knight also makes an incredible chocolate hearth bread, Pain Chocolate, that's worth waiting for all week.

Makes 2 dozen cookies

> 5 ounces semi-sweet chocolate
> 3 ounces bittersweet chocolate
> 6 tablespoons unsalted butter
> 1/3 cup all-purpose flour
> 1 teaspoon baking powder
> 1/4 teaspoon salt
> 2 eggs
> 2 teaspoons vanilla
> 1 tablespoon instant espresso powder
> 3/4 cup granulated sugar
> 3/4 cup semi-sweet chocolate chips
> 1/3 cup chopped pecans
> 1/3 cup chopped walnuts

Preheat oven to 325 degrees.

Melt the chocolate and butter in the top of a double boiler over hot water. Allow to cool slightly.

Sift together the flour, baking powder, and salt.

In a medium bowl, beat the eggs, vanilla, and espresso powder until well combined. Add the sugar and beat until pale and thick. Add the chocolate mixture and continue mixing 1 minute more.

Stir in the flour mixture until combined and then fold in the chocolate chips and nuts. Drop by rounded tablespoons onto ungreased baking sheets. Bake 13 to 15 minutes or until they rise slightly and form a thin crust. Cool on wire racks.

The White Swan Guest House, Mount Vernon, Washington

Chocolate Chip Cookies

These are the delightful chocolate chip cookies innkeeper Peter Goldfarb makes at The White Swan Guest House. They're great for munching while watching the geese and other waterfowl in the fields surrounding his wonderful inn on the outskirts of La Conner, WA.

Makes about 90 cookies

> 1 cup butter flavored Crisco
> 3/4 cup granulated sugar
> 3/4 cup firmly packed brown sugar
> 1 tablespoon vanilla
> 2 eggs
> 2 1/2 cups all-purpose flour
> 1 teaspoon baking soda
> 1 teaspoon salt
> 2 cups chocolate chips

Preheat oven to 375 degrees.

In the bowl of an electric mixer, cream the shortening with the white and brown sugars until light and fluffy. Beat in the vanilla. Add the eggs, one at a time, beating well after each addition.

In a small bowl, stir together the flour, baking soda, and salt. Add to the creamed mixture and stir to blend well. Stir in the chocolate chips. For extra-crisp cookies, chill the dough for 1 hour before baking.

Drop the dough, by teaspoonful, onto a baking sheet. Bake for about 8 minutes or until golden brown. Remove from oven and transfer to a wire rack to cool. Repeat with remaining dough.

"Everybody seems to have a never-ending appetite for chocolate. Culinary fads come and go, but chocolate remains. (It's) the flavor that beats all others."

– Craig Clairborne and Peter Franey, "Chocolate Mania," New York Times Magazine, 1984.

Hello Dolly Bars

Also known as Magic Bars or Seven Layer Bars, these cookie bars are so easy — and delicious — you can make them with young children.

Makes 24 bars

> 1/2 cup butter, melted
> 1 cup graham cracker crumbs
> 1 cup flaked coconut
> 1 cup semi-sweet chocolate chips
> 1 cup chopped pecans
> 1 cup sweetened condensed milk

Preheat oven to 350 degrees.

Pour the melted butter into a 9 by 9-inch baking pan. Evenly sprinkle the graham cracker crumbs over the butter. Sprinkle the coconut over the graham cracker crumbs. Add the chocolate chips and top with the pecan layer. Pour the sweetened condensed milk over the chocolate chip layer. Bake 25-30 minutes. Cool. Cut into 1 by 3-inch pieces.

Christopher Columbus brought cacao beans from the New World to King Ferdinand. The beans were overlooked in favor of the many other treasures he brought back.

The Hunt Club (Sorrento Hotel), Seattle, Washington

Double Chocolate Chunk Cookies

These Double Chocolate Chunk Cookies are rich, dense, and chewy. They also freeze well.

Makes 8 dozen cookies

1 pound 6 ounces semi-sweet chocolate
6 tablespoons butter
5 eggs
2 cups granulated sugar
1 teaspoon vanilla
1 cup sifted all-purpose flour
2 teaspoons baking powder
1 teaspoon salt
1 pound milk chocolate, chopped into small chunks
1 1/2 cups chopped nuts, any variety

Preheat oven to 350 degrees. Line cookie sheets with parchment paper.

Melt the semi-sweet chocolate and butter in a double boiler over hot water, stirring occasionally. Set aside to cool.

Place the eggs, sugar, and vanilla in a saucepan and heat over a low flame, whisking constantly, until warm to the touch. When warm, remove from heat and beat with a mixer until pale and fluffy.

Stir together the flour, baking powder, and salt and fold into the egg mixture. Gently fold the melted chocolate into the egg mixture. Fold in the chocolate chips and nuts.

Drop by rounded tablespoons onto parchment-lined baking sheets. Bake for 12-15 minutes or until done. Cool on wire racks.

Chocolate Poppers

Chef Cathy Lusk shares her recipe for these delectable Chocolate Poppers. Our recipe tester calls them "a sin, probably a mortal sin, but worth it!"

Makes 100 cookies

Almond Brownie:

8 ounces unsweetened chocolate

1 1/2 cups butter

3 cups granulated sugar

7 eggs

1/2 teaspoon salt

1 1/2 teaspoons almond extract

2 cups blanched almonds, ground

2 tablespoons instant espresso powder

Buttercream Frosting:

6 egg yolks

3/4 cup granulated sugar

1/2 cup corn syrup

1 pound butter, softened and lightly whipped with a fork

1/2 teaspoon almond extract

1/2 teaspoon vanilla

6 ounces bittersweet chocolate, melted

For Almond Brownies:

Preheat oven to 350 degrees. Butter and flour a 9 by 13-inch baking pan.

Melt the chocolate and butter together in the top of a double boiler over hot water. Cool slightly.

Stir the sugar into the chocolate mixture. Add the eggs, one at a time, beating well after each addition. Stir in the salt, almond extract, ground almonds, and espresso powder. Do not over mix.

Pour into prepared pan and bake about 35 minutes until the mixture is set up—it will be fudgy in the center. It is most important not to overbake! Cool.

For Buttercream Frosting:

In a medium bowl, beat the egg yolks with an electric mixer until pale yellow.

In a small saucepan, combine the sugar and corn syrup. Heat, stirring constantly, until it reaches a full boil. Immediately transfer to a glass measuring cup.

Using an electric mixer, beat the syrup into the egg yolks, being careful not to pour the syrup onto the beaters. Continue beating the mixture until it cools to the same temperature as the softened butter (about 5 minutes).

While beating constantly, add the softened butter, by tablespoons, to the cooled egg mixture. You should end up with a smooth mixture. If it curdles, it means your egg mixture is too warm or your butter is too cold. To remedy: Stir your curdled mix over a bowl of ice water just until it smoothes out. Immediately remove from ice water and beat in remaining butter.

Stir almond extract, vanilla, and melted chocolate into buttercream mixture. Do not refrigerate. The buttercream will store at room temperature for 2 days.

To Assemble: Cut cooled brownies into small circles (a donut hole cutter works well) and pipe buttercream frosting onto each circle. Or simply spread the buttercream over all the brownies and cut into small squares.

Serve about 5 poppers per person as a dessert.

> Cacoa pods (that contain the cacoa beans from which chocolate is made) grow right from the trunks and thick main branches of the cacoa tree.

Peppermint Brownies

Duck Soup is a wonderful restaurant on San Juan Island. Chef/owner Gretchen Allison serves this rich chocolate brownie layered with mint cream with her Vanilla Mint Ice Cream and Hot Fudge Sauce. Yummm!

Makes 16 brownies

> 1 cup plus 2 teaspoons butter, divided
> 7 ounces peppermint patties
> 2 eggs
> 3/4 cup granulated sugar
> 4 ounces semi-sweet chocolate
> 2 ounces unsweetened chocolate
> 1/4 cup chocolate syrup
> Pinch salt
> 1 teaspoon vanilla
> 1/2 cup all-purpose flour
> 1 1/4 cups chopped walnuts
> Vanilla mint ice cream (see recipe page 158)
> Hot fudge sauce (see recipe page 167)

Preheat oven to 350 degrees. Line a 7 by 10-inch baking pan as follows: Invert the pan and center a 15-inch length of aluminum foil, shiny side down, over the bottom of the pan. Shape the foil over the pan. Remove the foil. Turn the pan right side up and place the foil into the pan and press it into place. Place 2 teaspoons of butter in the foil-lined pan and put it into the oven to melt. Remove from oven when melted and brush the butter over the foil with a pastry brush.

Unwrap the peppermint patties and flatten between pieces of plastic wrap to twice their original size (1/2-inch thickness).

In a large bowl, beat the eggs and sugar until pale and thick.

Melt the remaining 1 cup butter, chocolates, syrup, and salt in the top of a double boiler over hot water. Add melted chocolate mixture and vanilla to the egg mixture and beat thoroughly.

Stir in the flour until well moistened and then stir in the walnuts.

Pour 1/2 of the brownie mixture into the prepared pan. Cover with the flattened peppermint patties. Spread remaining batter over the patties and bake for 30 minutes. Cool on wire rack. Remove foil and cut into 16 pieces.

To serve, place a brownie on a serving plate. Top with a scoop of vanilla mint ice cream and drizzle with hot fudge sauce.

Grateful Bread Bakery, Pacific City, Oregon
Cream Cheese Brownies

Laura Seide's Cream Cheese Brownies are one of this author's favorites. They're moist, dark chocolate brownies topped with a rich, cheesy topping.

Makes 24 brownies

Brownie Layer:

1 1/2 cup melted butter

3 cups granulated sugar

6 eggs

1 teaspoon vanilla

1 1/2 cups all-purpose flour

1 1/2 cups cocoa powder

Cream Cheese Layer:

2 8-ounce packages cream cheese

2 eggs

3/4 cup granulated sugar

2 tablespoons all-purpose flour

1 teaspoon vanilla

For Brownie Layer: Preheat oven to 350 degrees. Butter a 9 by 13-inch baking pan.

Combine the butter and sugar in the bowl of an electric mixer and beat well. Add the eggs 2 at a time, beating well after each addition. Beat in vanilla. Add flour and cocoa and stir to combine. Do not over mix.

For the Cream Cheese Layer: Place the cream cheese, eggs, sugar, flour, and vanilla in the bowl of a food processor and blend until smooth.

Pour most of the brownie layer into the prepared pan, reserving a small amount for topping.

Spread the cream cheese batter over the chocolate and smooth with a spatula. With a spoon, dollop 6 portions of the reserved chocolate batter onto the top of the cream cheese. Using the tip of a knife, swirl the chocolate topping into the cream cheese layer.

Bake 55 to 60 minutes. Cool completely in the pan before cutting.

> Brownies were invented in the 1920s, the result of a failed cake recipe.

Georgia's Bakery, La Conner, Washington
Georgia's Brownies

Locals in La Conner crowd Georgia's Bakery for her delightful baked goods. Try her easy-to-make, gooey and rich brownies.

Makes 20 brownies

For the Brownies:
1 1/4 cups sifted high-quality cocoa powder
2 1/2 cups granulated sugar
1 1/2 cups melted unsalted butter
1 tablespoon vanilla
6 eggs, beaten
1 cup plus 1 tablespoon all-purpose flour
Pinch salt
1 1/2 cups chopped walnuts

For the Ganache Topping:
1/2 cup plus 2 tablespoons whipping cream, divided
6 ounces semi-sweet chocolate chips
2 ounces white chocolate, chopped

Preheat oven to 350 degrees. Oil and flour a 9 by 13-inch baking pan.

In a large bowl, stir together the cocoa and sugar. Add the melted butter and blend well. Stir in the vanilla and then the eggs. Add the flour and salt and blend well. Stir in the walnuts. Pour into the prepared pan. Bake for 35 minutes or until the center puffs up slightly and the edges are obviously browned. Cool.

Scald 1/2 cup cream in a small pan. Pour over the chocolate chips and whisk until smooth.

In another small pan, scald the remaining cream. Pour over the chopped white chocolate and whisk until smooth.

When the brownies are completely cool, frost with dark chocolate ganache, then drizzle the white chocolate ganache diagonally over the tops of the brownies. Cut into 20 bars.

Whitman Samplers, famous for their old-fashioned "sampler" boxes and pictured index to each chocolate, first appeared in 1912. They're still popular today.

Paley's Place, Portland, Oregon

Hot Pecan Brownies

These Hot Pecan Brownies are one of pastry chef Jennifer Flanagan's signature desserts. They're rich with a deep chocolate flavor and the pecans add a delightful counterpoint to the soft brownie.

Makes 9 servings

Syrup:
3/4 cup firmly packed brown sugar
1/4 cup unsweetened cocoa powder
2 tablespoons coffee extract
Pinch of salt
3/4 cup water
3/4 cup whipping cream
1 1/2 tablespoons vanilla

Brownie:
1 cup all-purpose flour
3/4 cup granulated sugar
1/4 cup unsweetened cocoa powder
2 teaspoons baking powder
1/2 teaspoon salt
1/2 cup buttermilk
1/4 cup melted butter
3/4 teaspoon vanilla
1 cup toasted pecan pieces

For Syrup: Combine the brown sugar, cocoa, coffee extract, salt, water, cream, and vanilla in a small saucepan. Heat over medium heat until tiny bubbles form around the edges of the pan. Set aside.

For Brownie: Preheat oven to 350 degrees. Butter an 8 by 8-inch baking pan.

Sift the flour, sugar, cocoa, baking powder, and salt into a large mixing bowl. Add the buttermilk, melted butter, vanilla, and pecans. Blend until just combined. Pour the mixture into the prepared baking pan and pour the reserved syrup over the brownie. Bake for about 25 minutes or until the center is firm to the touch. Cool completely.

To Serve: Cut brownies into 9 servings. Place a brownie on a serving plate and spoon some of the sauce over. Serve with Caramel Ice Cream (see page 163).

Belgian Chocolate Walnut Fudge Brownies

At Birchfield Manor Country Inn in Yakima, Washington, pastry chef Greg Massett's Belgian Chocolate Walnut Fudge Brownies are often on the dinner menu. They're so rich and gooey, you only need a small serving.

Makes 24-30 brownies

Brownie:

2 cups plus 2 tablespoons granulated sugar

1 1/2 cup butter

5 medium eggs

6 tablespoons unsweetened cocoa powder

2 cups pastry flour

1 1/2 cups walnuts, coarsely chopped

8 ounces chopped Belgian chocolate

White Chocolate Ganache:

16 ounces chopped white chocolate

3/4 cup whipping cream

Dark Chocolate Ganache:

8 ounces chopped bittersweet chocolate

1/2 cup plus 2 tablespoons whipping cream

Preheat oven to 350 degrees. Line a 10 by 13-inch baking pan with parchment paper.

Cream together the butter and sugar with an electric mixer. Blend in eggs one at a time.

Sift together cocoa powder and pastry flour. Add to butter and sugar mixture and blend until just incorporated. Mix in walnuts and chopped chocolate.

Bake 20-25 minutes until the edges are firm and center slightly soft.

In a saucepan, heat 3/4 cup whipping cream until bubbles form around the edges. Remove from heat. Add chopped white chocolate and whisk until chocolate is melted and smooth. Cool slightly.

> One ounce of cocoa or baking chocolate contains 10 percent of the Recommended Daily Allowance (RDA) of iron.

In another saucepan, heat the 1/2 cup plus 2 tablespoons cream until bubbles form around the edges. Remove from heat and add the chopped bittersweet chocolate. Whisk until chocolate is melted and smooth.

When brownies are completely cool and ganaches are slightly cool, frost the brownies with white ganache. Drizzle dark chocolate horizontally over white ganache. Cut into squares.

Pies & Tarts

Pies and tarts evoke images
of home and hearth.
These chocolate pies and tarts
are homey with a touch
of sophistication.

The Brewery, Grants Pass, Oregon
Chocolate Peanut Butter Pie

There's something magical about the combination of chocolate and peanut butter. This wonderfully creamy version of Chocolate Peanut Butter Pie served at The Brewery Restaurant in Grants Pass is made at their bakery, Chocolate Affair.

Makes 1 9-inch pie

Chocolate Crust:
> 2 cups chocolate cookie crumbs **
> 1/4 cup melted butter

Peanut Butter Filling:
> 1 cup creamy peanut butter
> 1 8-ounce package cream cheese
> 3/4 cup powdered sugar
> 1 teaspoon melted butter
> 1/2 teaspoon vanilla
> 2/3 cup whipping cream

Chocolate Glaze:
> 2 teaspoons whipping cream
> 1 teaspoon corn syrup
> 1/2 teaspoon instant espresso powder
> 1 tablespoon water
> 2 ounces semi-sweet chocolate

** Nabisco Famous Chocolate Wafers™ work well.

For Crust: In a medium bowl, combine the cookie crumbs and melted butter. Press onto the bottom and up the sides of a 9-inch pie pan. Bake at 350 degrees for 7-10 minutes.

For Filling: In a large bowl with an electric mixer, beat the peanut butter with the cream cheese until smooth. Add the sugar, butter, and vanilla and beat 2 to 3 minutes.

In a separate bowl, whip the cream until soft peaks form. Fold about 1/4 of the whipped cream into the peanut butter mixture. When well combined, fold in the remaining whipped cream. Pour into prepared crust and chill for several hours.

For Glaze: In a small saucepan, over low heat, stir together the cream, corn syrup, espresso powder, and water. Bring to a simmer. Add the chocolate and whisk until smooth. Cool slightly and spread on top of chilled pie. Using a pastry bag fitted with a small plain tip, pipe remaining chocolate glaze around edge of pie to garnish.

Prospector Pies, Wenatchee, Washington
Tollhouse Cookie Pie

With more that 25 different varieties of pie, the bakers at Prospector Pies in Wenatchee know how to make great pie. This easy-as-pie recipe yields a crispy top like pecan pie with a gooey, chocolatey bottom. If you like warm Tollhouse cookies, you'll love this one.

Makes 1 9-inch pie

> 2 eggs
> 1 cup margarine, melted
> 1/2 cup granulated sugar
> 1/2 cup firmly packed brown sugar
> 1/2 cup all-purpose flour
> 1 cup semi-sweet chocolate chips
> 1 cup chopped walnuts
> 1 unbaked 9-inch pastry shell
> Vanilla ice cream, optional

Preheat oven to 350 degrees.

In a large bowl with an electric mixer, beat the eggs until they are light and frothy. Add the margarine and mix well. Beat in the white and brown sugar. Stir in the flour.

Add the chocolate chips and walnuts and stir by hand to combine. Pour into the unbaked pie shell and bake uncovered for 25 minutes. Cover with an inverted pie tin and continue baking for another 25 to 30 minutes. The pie should be set in the center.

Serve warm with vanilla ice cream, if desired.

Recipe Tester's Note: If you're in a hurry or not handy at making crust, use a ready-made crust. Or use the recipe that follows.

Pie Pastry
> 1 cup all-purpose flour
> 1/2 teaspoon salt
> 1/3 cup plus 1 tablespoon shortening
> 2-3 tablespoons cold water

Place flour and salt into a bowl and cut in shortening thoroughly. Sprinkle with water, 1 tablespoon at a time. Mix until the flour is moistened and the dough comes clean off the sides of the bowl (you may need to add 1-2 teaspoons more water).

Gather dough into a ball. Pat onto a lightly-floured surface. Roll dough about 2 inches larger than 9" pie pan. Fold dough into quarters and ease into pie pan. Trim excess dough. Use a fork to flatten pastry evenly around rim. Or flute by pinching the rim using the right index finger on the inside of the pastry rim, the left thumb and index finger on the outside. Pinch into small "v" shapes.

Wild Garlic, Bellingham, Washington
Chocolate Peanut Butter Pie

This Chocolate Peanut Butter Pie from Wild Garlic in Bellingham, Washington, is silky with a smooth, rich ganache topping.

Makes 1 10-inch pie

Crust:
    1 cup graham cracker crumbs
    1 cup chocolate cookie crumbs **
    1/2 cup chopped peanuts
    1/3 cup unsalted butter, melted
    1 tablespoon vanilla
    1 tablespoon dark rum, optional

Filling:
    2 cups whipping cream
    1 tablespoon vanilla
    2 8-ounce packages cream cheese, softened
    1 cup granulated sugar
    2 cups crunchy peanut butter
    1/4 cup melted butter

Ganache:
    4 ounces bittersweet chocolate (preferably Belgian chocolate)
    3/4 cup whipping cream

Garnish:
    chopped peanuts
    cocoa powder

** Nabisco Famous Chocolate Wafers™ work well.

For Crust: Spray a 10-inch springform pan with non-stick cooking spray.

Combine the graham cracker crumbs, cookie crumbs, peanuts, melted butter, vanilla, and dark rum, if using, in the bowl of a food processor. Process until well combined. Mixture should be just moist enough to hold together. Add a little more butter, if necessary. Press the crumb mixture onto the bottom and up the sides of the prepared pan. Take care to keep the thickness of the crumb mixture even on the bottom and sides.

For Filling: In a large bowl with an electric mixer, whip the whipping cream with the vanilla until soft peaks form. Set aside

In another large bowl with an electric mixer, beat together the cream cheese and sugar. Add the peanut butter and butter and blend thoroughly. Blend in the whipped cream and pour into the prepared crust. Refrigerate overnight or freeze.

For Ganache: In a small saucepan, combine the chocolate and cream. Heat over low heat, stirring constantly, until the chocolate is melted and the mixture is smooth. The chocolate will thicken and become dark and glossy.

Place the chilled pie on a cookie sheet and pour the hot ganache over the top. Tip the pie to cover the top and drizzle down the sides. Let cool.

For Garnish: Garnish with chopped peanuts and cocoa powder and serve.

In an interview with *Time* magazine, veteran actress Katherine Hepburn said, "What you see before you is the result of a lifetime of eating chocolate." Those in the know say Ms. Hepburn's favorite chocolate passion is dark, pudding-like brownies.

Home Fires Bakery, Leavenworth, Washington
Chocolate Mint Truffle Pie

Think you don't like mint? Think again. This Chocolate Mint Truffle Pie is light, refreshing, and delightfully rich. You can serve it as a pie or in individual cupcake or candy paper cups.

Makes 1 9-inch pie

Crust:
>1/4 cup chocolate wafer crumbs (about 4 or 5 chocolate wafer cookies) **
>
>6 tablespoons vanilla wafer crumbs (about 7 vanilla wafers)
>
>2 tablespoons melted butter

Filling:
>1/2 envelope unflavored gelatin (1 teaspoon)
>
>1/4 cup water
>
>1 1/2 teaspoons peppermint extract
>
>6 tablespoons semi-sweet chocolate chips
>
>1 8-ounce package cream cheese
>
>1 cup granulated sugar
>
>1 cup whipping cream
>
>1 1/2 teaspoons vanilla

Topping:
>3 tablespoons semi-sweet chocolate chips

>** Nabisco Famous Chocolate Wafers™ work well.

Preheat oven to 300 degrees.

For Crust: Stir together the chocolate and vanilla crumbs and the butter. Pat evenly onto the bottom and up the sides of a 9-inch pie pan. Bake for 5 minutes. Set aside to cool.

For Filling: Melt the chocolate in the top of a double boiler. Set aside to cool.

Soften the gelatin in the water, let stand for 5 minutes. Heat over low heat until clear and then add the peppermint extract and stir well. Add the gelatin mixture to the melted chocolate and blend.

Meanwhile, in a large mixing bowl, beat cream cheese until fluffy. Add the sugar and beat again until fluffy.

> In England during the reign of William and Mary (1690), one had to have a license to sell drinking chocolate.

Add the chocolate mixture to the cream cheese mixture and blend well. Set aside.

In a large bowl, whip the cream until soft peaks form. Add the vanilla and beat until firm peaks form. Fold the whipped cream into the chocolate mixture and pour into the prepared piecrust. Smooth with a spatula. Chill until set.

For Topping: Melt the chocolate and drizzle in an attractive pattern over the top of the pie. Chill to set. Pie can be frozen and served directly from the freezer.

Recipe Tester's note: We serve this wonderful dessert in tiny foil candy cups right out of the freezer. It makes an elegant dessert.

John Horan's Steak and Seafood House, Wenatchee, Washington

Aurora Tart

The Aurora Tart is this author's favorite dessert at John Horan's Steak and Seafood House. It has a thin, flaky crust that's topped with layers of caramel, chocolate, whipping cream, and chopped, toasted almonds.

Makes 1 10-inch tart

Crust:

1 3/4 cups all-purpose flour

1/4 cup granulated sugar

12 tablespoons cold butter, cut into pieces

2 egg yolks

1/4 cup whipping cream

Filling:

3 cups whipping cream

1 3/4 cups granulated sugar

2 tablespoons water

3 tablespoons butter

1/4 teaspoon salt

4 egg yolks

1 egg

1st Topping:

2 ounces bittersweet chocolate, chopped

1/4 cup whipping cream

Pralines:

2 tablespoons soft butter

1 cup granulated sugar

1/2 cup whole almonds, toasted (see note)

Final Topping:

1 cup whipping cream

Preheat oven to 375 degrees.

For Crust: Combine the flour and sugar in the bowl of a food processor. Add cold butter and pulse until crumbly and butter pieces are the size of tiny peas. Add the yolks and cream and process a few seconds until the dough just comes together (dough will be very soft and grainy). Refrigerate for 15 minutes.

Roll dough out on a lightly-floured board and place in a 10-inch tart pan with removable bottom. Trim edges. Freeze for 30 minutes.

Line the tart shell with foil and fill with pie weights or dry beans. Bake for 30 minutes or until sides are set. Remove foil and pie weights and continue baking until light golden brown, about 5 to 7 minutes more. Cool on wire rack and set aside.

For Filling: Reduce oven to 325 degrees.

In a heavy-bottomed saucepan, heat the cream until hot and bubbles form around the edges.

In another heavy-bottomed saucepan, heat the sugar with 2 tablespoons of water until it melts and turns a honey caramel color. Remove from heat and slowly pour the hot cream into the caramel, stirring constantly. Be careful as the mixture will boil up. Stir until well blended. Return to medium heat and add butter and salt. Set aside.

> Nearly half of all the world's cacoa beans come from Brazil and the Ivory Coast of Africa.

In a large bowl, beat the egg yolks and egg until blended. Slowly whisk the caramel mixture into the eggs. Pour the filling into the baked shell and bake for 30 to 35 minutes or until set. Remove from oven and cool on a wire rack.

For 1st Topping: Heat the cream to boiling and pour over chopped chocolate. Stir until the chocolate is melted. Pour over the baked caramel custard and refrigerate.

For Pralines: Lightly butter a foil pie pan with the softened butter. Place the toasted almonds in the pie pan.

In a heavy-bottomed saucepan, heat the sugar, stirring, until it melts and turns a honey caramel color. Pour the caramel over the almonds and cool completely.

For Final Topping: Put the pralines in the bowl of a food processor and process until fine crumbs. Set aside.

Whip the whipping cream until stiff peaks form. Stir in half of the praline powder. Spread the whipped cream mixture over the tart. Sprinkle the remaining pralines over the tart.

Recipe Tester's note: To toast almonds, spread nuts on a baking sheet and roast at 350 degrees for 10 to 15 minutes, stirring occasionally.

Chocolate Bourbon Pecan Tart

At Coho Grill, chef Vern Liebelt serves this nutty chocolate tart warm. It has a crisp tart shell with a buttery layer of chocolate filling that's stuffed with pecans.

Makes 1 10-inch tart

Tart Shell:
1 1/4 cups cake flour
1/2 teaspoon granulated sugar
1/8 teaspoon salt
1/2 cup chilled unsalted butter
3 to 4 tablespoons ice water

Filling:
4 ounces chopped chocolate
3 eggs
1/2 cup melted butter
3/4 cup granulated sugar
1/2 cup firmly packed brown sugar
3/4 cup light corn syrup
1 tablespoon bourbon
1 teaspoon vanilla
1/2 teaspoon salt
1 cup pecan halves

For Tart Shell: Combine the flour, sugar, and salt in the bowl of a food processor. Cut the butter into 8 pieces and add to the flour mixture. Pulse the food processor 4 or 5 times or until the butter is cut into the flour to resemble tiny peas. Add the water and pulse 1 or 2 times to just barely combine. Turn out of food processor and form into a ball. Wrap in plastic wrap and refrigerate for 1 hour.

Remove pastry from refrigerator and let warm for a few minutes to make rolling easier. Roll out on a lightly floured surface and fit into a 10-inch tart pan. Leave the sides of pastry a little higher than the sides of the pan as the pastry will shrink a little during baking. Set aside.

In 1931, Ruth Wakefield invented the first chocolate chip cookie. At her Tollhouse Restaurant in Whitman, Massachusetts, Ruth chopped up a semisweet chocolate bar and put it into a batch of cookies. She sold the rights to her Tollhouse™ cookie to the Nestlé Company and the rest is history.

For Filling: In the top of a double boiler, melt the chocolate over hot, not boiling, water. Stir until smooth. Let cool.

In a large bowl, beat together the eggs, butter, white and brown sugars, corn syrup, bourbon, vanilla, and salt. Add the melted chocolate and stir to combine. Refrigerate until ready to use. (Filling can be held in refrigerator for up to two weeks.)

To Bake Tart: Preheat oven to 350 degrees.

Arrange the pecan halves in the bottom of the tart shell. Pour filling into tart shell and bake for 45 to 50 minutes or until the filling is firm but not hard. Do not overcook. Remove from oven and cool on a wire rack.

Luna Restaurant, Spokane, Washington
Macadamia Nut Chocolate Chip Tart

This is Luna's version of Tollhouse pie. The crust is melt-in-the-mouth flaky and the center has a wonderful combination of chocolate and nut flavors.

Makes 1 9-inch tart

Crust:

2 cups all-purpose flour
7 tablespoons granulated sugar
3/4 cup cold unsalted butter, cut into bits
1/2 teaspoon vanilla

Filling:

3/4 cup unsalted butter, softened
2 eggs
1/2 cup granulated sugar
1/2 cup all-purpose flour
1/4 teaspoon salt
1 tablespoon vanilla
6 ounces semi-sweet chocolate chips
1 cup macadamia nuts, coarsely chopped

For Crust: Preheat oven to 350 degrees.

Combine the flour, sugar, butter, and vanilla in the bowl of a food processor. Process until mixed. Dough will be crumbly like cornmeal.

Press into a 9" springform pan.

For Filling: In a large bowl with an electric mixer, beat the butter until light, add the eggs and beat well. Mix in the sugar, flour, salt, and vanilla. Stir in the chocolate chips and macadamia nuts by hand.

Pour into the prepared tart shell and bake for 45 minutes or until set. Serve warm.

> In 1939, the Nestlé Company sold the first chocolate chips. Today they produce more than 250 million chocolate chips every day.

Recipe Tester's note: You can use a 9-inch tart pan, but the springform pan makes this tart easier to remove from the pan.

*"Giving chocolate
to others is an
ultimate form of
communication,
a sharing of deep,
dark secrets."*

*— Milton Zelman,
publisher of
Chocolate News*

Pudding, Mousse, & Crème Brulee

They can be smooth and thick, rich
and cake-like, or light and crispy.
Served warm or cold, creamy
pudding-type desserts offer a
wide range of wonderful textures
and taste sensations.

Decadence Café and Catering, Victoria, B.C.

White Chocolate
Cappuccino Crème Brulee

This is a rich, silky crème custard with a crunchy, sweet espresso and brown sugar topping.

Makes 6 servings

Custard:

    10 egg yolks
    2 cups whipping cream
    1 cup milk
    1/4 cup granulated sugar
    6 ounces finely chopped white chocolate (preferably Callebaut or Tobler)
    1 teaspoon vanilla
    1 teaspoon instant coffee powder
    1 tablespoon dark rum

Topping:

    1/3 cup firmly packed brown sugar
    1 teaspoon instant espresso powder

Preheat oven to 350 degrees.

Place the egg yolks in a large bowl and lightly blend. Set aside.

In a large saucepan, combine the cream, milk, sugar, vanilla, instant coffee, and rum and heat over medium heat until the sugar dissolves. Add the chopped chocolate and stir until melted. Do not boil.

Slowly pour the hot cream mixture into the egg yolks, whisking constantly. Whisk until well combined. Pour into 6 4-ounce ramekins or custard cups. Place the ramekins in a large baking pan and pour boiling water around the ramekins until the water level reaches 2/3 up the sides of the cups. Bake for 1 hour.

Combine the topping ingredients in a small bowl, stir to blend. Sprinkle the topping over the custard and place under broiler for 1-2 minutes until bubbly and brown. Refrigerate 8 hours or overnight before serving. Serve cold, room termperature, or warm.

Carob isn't real chocolate. It's the mashed fruit of a Mediterranean pine tree. One tablespoon of carob has the same calories as one tablespoon of cocoa.

Wildflowers Restaurant, Mount Vernon, Washington
Chocolate Mousse

This delightful mousse recipe is simple, yet your guests will think you're a gourmet cook. The loganberry liqueur and port add a rich complexity to this dessert that will have guests clamoring for another serving and a copy of the recipe.

Makes 8 servings

> 8 ounces semi-sweet chocolate, chopped (preferably Callebaut)
> 4 tablespoons butter
> 1/2 cup espresso or very strong coffee
> 1/3 cup Whidbey's Loganberry Liqueur
> 1/4 cup Whidbey's Port
> 3/4 cup whipping cream
> 5 egg whites

Combine the chocolate, butter and espresso in the top of a double boiler over simmering water. Heat, stirring occasionally, over medium heat until chocolate is melted and mixture is smooth. Remove double boiler from heat. Stir in liqueur and port. Cool to 90 degrees.

In a medium bowl, whip the cream until soft peaks form. Set aside.

In another medium bowl, beat the egg whites until soft peaks form.

Beat the chocolate mixture into the whipped cream. Fold the egg whites into the chocolate mixture 1/3 at a time, folding carefully until well combined.

Spoon into 8 dessert glasses and chill for several hours before serving.

Note: See raw egg caution, page 18.

Le Crocodile, Vancouver, B.C.

Chocolate Mousse

This chocolate mousse derives its rich, unusual flavor and toothsome texture from ground hazelnut praline and ground toasted almonds. If you want a less chunky texture, pound the praline into powder.

Makes 8 servings

> 7 ounces chopped dark chocolate
> 3 1/3 ounces toasted sliced almonds, finely ground
> 2 ounces ground hazelnut praline (see note)
> 2 cups whipping cream
> 9 egg whites
> 1/2 cup granulated sugar
> Sweetened whipped cream for garnish
> Mint sprigs for garnish
> Whole toasted hazelnuts for garnish

In the top of a double boiler, melt the chocolate over hot, not boiling, water.

While the chocolate is melting, stir together the almonds and hazelnut praline. Stir in the melted chocolate. Cool.

In a large chilled bowl, whip the cream until medium peaks form. Fold into the cooled chocolate mixture.

In another bowl, whip the egg whites until stiff, but not dry. Add sugar to stiffen the whites. Gently fold into the chocolate mixture until completely incorporated.

Pipe the mousse into 8 serving glasses and refrigerate overnight. Garnish with whipped cream, a mint sprig and a whole hazelnut.

Note: See raw egg caution, page 18.

Recipe Tester's note: Hazelnut praline is available at fine specialty food stores. Or use the following recipe.

Hazelnut Praline
> 1 cup roasted, skinned hazelnuts
> 1/2 cup granulated sugar
> 2 tablespoons water

Butter a cookie sheet.

In a small, heavy saucepan or skillet, heat sugar and water. Swirl gently from time to time until the sugar and water come to a boil. Reduce heat to medium-high, cover pan, and continue boiling for 2 minutes. Uncover pan and boil for another 2 minutes, without stirring, until sugar turns a deep golden color. Watch carefully as sugar syrup burns quickly. Immediately remove from heat and stir in hazelnuts. Turn the mixture onto the buttered cookie sheet and spread as thinly as possible. Cool until hardened.

For chunky praline, place cooled praline in a heavy plastic bag and pound bag with heavy spoon, mallet, or rolling pin. For praline powder, keep pounding until the praline becomes a powder. Or place cooled praline into a food processor and grind into a powder.

> Many people incorrectly assume that Baby Ruth candy bars were named for the famous baseball player Babe Ruth. They were named for President Grover Cleveland's youngest daughter, Ruth.

Serafina, Seattle, Washington

Mousse di Chocolata

Serafina's Mousse di Chocolata is a hearty, chunky mousse that has a satisfying deep chocolate flavor.

Makes 6 servings

> 8 ounces semi-sweet chocolate
> 3 tablespoons espresso
> 3 eggs, separated
> 2 tablespoons brandy
> 1/2 cup plus 1 heaping teaspoon granulated sugar, divided
> 1 teaspoon vanilla
> 3/4 cup whipping cream
> Whipped cream and chocolate shavings for garnish

Place the chocolate in the top of a double boiler over simmering water. Heat over medium heat until chocolate is melted.

Place the egg yolks in a medium bowl and the egg whites in another medium bowl. To the yolks add the brandy, 1/2 cup sugar, and vanilla. Beat on medium speed until thick and pale yellow.

Add the heaping teaspoon sugar to the egg whites. Using clean beaters, beat until stiff peaks form.

When the chocolate is completely melted, transfer it to a chilled mixing bowl and add the espresso. Stir with a spatula until the espresso is incorporated and some chocolate bits have formed. Fold in the yolk mixture. When the yolks are thoroughly incorporated, fold in the egg whites.

In a large bowl, whip the cream until soft peaks form. Fold into the mousse mixture and transfer the mousse to a clean bowl. Chill for several hours.

To serve, spoon mousse into dessert glasses and garnish with additional whipped cream and chocolate shavings.

Note: See raw egg caution, page 18.

> Role Reversal:
> On Valentine's Day,
> it's Japanese girls
> who give their boy-
> friends chocolate.

Apple Cellar Bakery and Rotisserie, Ashland, Oregon

White Chocolate Grand Marnier Mousse Cups

Ashland's Apple Cellar Bakery is a sophisticated from-scratch bakery specializing in delightful European pastries, cakes, rolls, and breads. Their White Chocolate Grand Marnier Mousse has a delicate texture with a hint of orange flavoring.

Makes 8 servings

White Chocolate Ganache:

1 pound chopped white chocolate

3/4 cup whipping cream

5 tablespoons unsalted butter

Grand Marnier Mousse:

3 tablespoons Grand Marnier

2 tablespoons orange flavored coffee syrup (or Tia Maria Liqueur)

1 teaspoon vanilla

1/4 teaspoon orange extract

Grated peel of 1 orange

1 envelope unflavored gelatin

2 cups whipping cream

2 tablespoons granulated sugar

Shaved white and dark chocolate for garnish

For White Chocolate Ganache: In the top of a double boiler, melt the chocolate over hot, not boiling, water.

In small saucepan, heat the butter and cream until the butter melts. Remove from heat and whisk melted white chocolate into melted butter mixture. Let stand for 10 minutes then whisk until smooth. Keep warm.

For Grand Marnier Mousse: In a small saucepan, stir together the Grand Marnier, orange syrup, vanilla, orange extract, orange peel, and gelatin. Let stand 5 minutes to soften the gelatin. Heat over low flame until gelatin is dissolved. Let cool.

Whip the cream and sugar until soft peaks form. With mixer at low speed, add cooled gelatin mixture, and mix until just combined. Fold the white chocolate ganache into the whipped cream mixture with a rubber spatula. Transfer immediately to serving cups. Garnish with shaved white and dark chocolate.

Malted White Chocolate Mousse

This is an easy recipe from Skamania Lodge's pastry chef, Kristen Woods. It yields a light, creamy mousse. The chocolate cups make for an elegant presentation.

Makes 6 servings

> 1/2 envelope unflavored gelatin
> 2 tablespoons cold water
> 3/4 cup whipping cream, divided
> 7 tablespoons plus 2 teaspoons granulated sugar
> 3 tablespoons malted milk powder
> 3 3/4 ounces white chocolate, melted
> 3 ounces semi-sweet chocolate, melted
> Whipped cream for garnish
> Chocolate shavings for garnish

In a small bowl, combine the gelatin and cold water. Let stand for about 5 minutes to soften.

In a small saucepan over medium heat, heat 1/4 cup whipping cream until bubbles form around the edge of the pan. Add the softened gelatin to the hot cream and stir to dissolve the gelatin.

In a chilled bowl with chilled beaters, whip the remaining cream with the sugar and malted milk powder until soft peaks form.

Stir the gelatin mixture into the melted white chocolate and gently fold into the whipped cream. Chill until set.

Brush melted semi-sweet chocolate inside 6 small waxed paper cups. Chill briefly and repeat with two more coats of melted chocolate in each cup. Chill between each coat.

> Chocolate bars were invented during the 19th century. They extracted cocoa butter from cacao beans and mixed the cocoa butter with sugar into a thin paste and molded it into bar-like shapes. Voila! Portable chocolate!

To remove the chocolate cups from the paper cups, lightly scrape any drips of chocolate from the lip of the cups with the back of a paring knife. Then, gently press the bottom of the cup and the chocolate cup should pop right out.

Using a pastry bag with a large, straight tip, pipe the white chocolate mousse into the chocolate cups, filling about 2/3 full. Garnish with whipped cream and shaved chocolate.

Bella Union Restaurant, Jacksonville, Oregon

Dark Chocolate and White Chocolate Mousse

The light, ultra-creamy texture of these mousses invites another bite. And another and another.

Makes 8 servings

> 1/2 pound bittersweet chocolate, grated
> 10 tablespoons butter, divided
> 6 egg yolks, divided
> 12 egg whites, divided
> 4 cups whipping cream
> 1/2 to 1 ounce Kahlua
> 1/2 ounce Grand Marnier
> 3/4 pound white chocolate, grated
> 1 ounce light rum

For Dark Chocolate Mousse: Place grated bittersweet chocolate and 5 tablespoons butter in a medium bowl over simmering water, stirring occasionally, until melted.

Add 3 egg yolks to the melted chocolate and stir well with a wire whip and set aside.

Place 6 egg whites in a large bowl and whip until stiff peaks form. Set aside.

In a chilled bowl with chilled beaters, whip 2 cups whipping cream with the Kahlua and Grand Marnier until stiff peaks form. Fold the whipped cream into the egg whites and then fold in the chocolate mixture until well combined. Chill.

For White Chocolate Mousse: Place the grated white chocolate and 5 tablespoons butter in a medium bowl over simmering water, stirring occasionally, until melted.

Add the remaining 3 egg yolks and stir well with a wire whip. Set aside.

Place the remaining 6 egg whites in a large bowl and whip until stiff peaks form. Set aside.

In a chilled bowl with chilled beaters, whip the remaining 2 cups whipping cream with the rum until stiff peaks form. Fold the whipped cream into the beaten egg whites and then fold in the white chocolate mixture until well combined. Chill.

To Assemble: Fill tall glasses with alternate layers of dark and white chocolate mousse, repeating until glasses are full. Garnish with whipped cream and shaved chocolate.

Note: See raw egg caution, page 18.

The Hunt Club (Sorrento Hotel), Seattle, Washington

Dark Chocolate Crème Brulee

This easy-to-make recipe yields a richly dark chocolate custard that's sure to be a hit with chocophiles. For a small family, cut the recipe in half.

Makes 8 servings

1/3 plus 1/2 cup granulated sugar, divided
6 egg yolks
1/2 cup milk
2 1/4 cups whipping cream
8 ounces melted dark chocolate

Preheat oven to 275 degrees. Butter 8 custard cups or ramekins.

In a medium bowl, whisk together 1/3 cup sugar and the egg yolks.

In a heavy-bottomed saucepan, combine the milk and cream. Sprinkle the remaining 1/2 cup sugar over the cream. Heat the mixture over medium heat until tiny bubbles form around the edges of the pan. Pour over melted chocolate and mix well.

Pour a small amount of the chocolate mixture into the egg yolk mixture and mix well. Pour the egg yolk mixture back into the chocolate mixture and stir until well combined. Strain.

Pour the mixture into the buttered custard cups and place the custard cups in a large baking pan. Pour boiling water around the custard cups until the water reaches half way up the sides of the cups. Bake for 45-55 minutes or until the custard is firm in the center. Serve warm.

> During World War II, the U.S. government commissioned the Hershey Company to develop a candy bar that soldiers could carry with them into battle. At times, Hershey Chocolate Bars were the only food the soldiers had to eat.

Cheri Walker's 42nd St. Café, Seaview, Washington
Chocolate Chip Crème Brulee

Our recipe tester served this creamy, lace-topped custard at a 4th of July picnic and got rave reviews.

Makes 4 servings (large custard cups) or 6-7 servings (standard 6 ounce custard cups)

> 5 egg yolks
> 1/2 cup plus 2 tablespoons granulated sugar, divided
> 2 cups whipping cream
> 1 tablespoon vanilla
> 1 teaspoon finely ground espresso beans
> 2 tablespoons semi-sweet chocolate chips

Preheat oven to 300 degrees.

In a large oven-proof bowl, whisk the yolks with 1/2 cup sugar.

In a small, heavy-bottomed saucepan, heat the cream until it just simmers. Slowly whisk the hot cream into the yolks. Add the vanilla and espresso coffee and mix well.

Place 1/2 teaspoon chocolate chips into each of the custard cups. Divide the dessert evenly between the custard cups and place in a baking pan. Pour boiling water into the baking pan until it reaches halfway up the sides of the custard cups.

Bake for 50-60 minutes or until the custard is set in the center. Remove cups from water and cool. Refrigerate.

To serve, sprinkle 1/2 tablespoon sugar over each custard. Broil until the sugar is browned, about 2 minutes. Cool several minutes before serving.

Fleuri Restaurant (The Sutton Place Hotel), Vancouver, B.C.

Triple Chocolate Croissant Pudding

Every Thursday, Friday, and Saturday nights, the Fleuri Restaurant hosts its famous Chocoholic Bar. With more than a dozen chocolate desserts to sample, it's hard to pick a favorite. The Triple Chocolate Croissant Pudding is rich with buttery croissants and bits of milk, white, and semi-sweet chocolate.

Makes 6 servings

> 6 cups milk
> 3/4 cup granulated sugar
> 5 eggs
> 4 cups cubed croissants (1-1 1/2 inch cubes)
> 1/3 cup milk chocolate chips
> 1/3 cup white chocolate chips
> 1/3 cup semi-sweet chocolate chips

Preheat oven to 350 degrees. Butter an 8-inch cake pan (needs to be at least 2 inches high).

In a large bowl, combine the milk and sugar. Add the eggs and beat until well combined. Place the cubed croissants in the prepared cake pan and pour the milk mixture over the croissants. Fold in the chocolate chips.

Place the cake pan in a large baking pan and pour boiling water around the cake pan to reach half way up the sides of the pan. Bake for 45 minutes or until set in the center. Serve warm.

> "Dutching," is a process of squeezing out some of the cocoa butter to make cocoa smoother.

Fleuri Restaurant (The Sutton Place Hotel), Vancouver, B.C.

White Chocolate Bavaroise

Another favorite from Fleuri's Chocoholic Bar, this White Chocolate Bavaroise has a texture that's a cross between a pudding and a mousse and a delicately soft white chocolate flavor.

Makes 8 servings

> Nonstick vegetable spray
> Powdered sugar
> 1 cup milk
> 4 ounces white chocolate, shaved or finely chopped
> 2 egg yolks
> 2 tablespoons plus 2 teaspoons granulated sugar
> 4 gelatin leaves or 2 envelopes unflavored gelatin
> 1/4 cup cold water
> 1 1/2 cups cream
> Fresh berries for garnish
> Chocolate leaves for garnish (see page 24)

Spray an 8-inch bowl with vegetable spray and sprinkle with powdered sugar, tapping out any excess sugar.

In a bowl, combine the sugar and egg yolks. In a small saucepan, bring the milk to a simmer. Slowly pour the milk into the egg-sugar mixture whisking constantly. Pour the mixture back into the saucepan and continue whisking over low heat until the mixture thickens (mixture will coat the back of a spoon.) Take off the heat and strain through a cheesecloth (to remove any egg that has cooked). Add the white chocolate and whisk to melt. Soak the gelatin in cold water until softened. Add softened gelatin to hot milk mixture and stir to dissolve. Cool.

Whip cream to soft peaks. Fold whipped cream into cooled milk mixture. Pour into prepared bowl and refrigerate overnight or until set.

To serve, unmold bavaroise onto a serving platter. Decorate with fresh berries and chocolate leaves.

Chez Shea, Seattle, Washington

Chocolate Steamed Pudding with Brandied Cherries

This dessert takes some time, but if you love chocolate steamed pudding, it's worth the effort. Chez Shea's signature warm Chocolate Steamed Pudding has a soft cake-like texture that's punctuated by chewy, sweet-sour cherries.

Makes 11 servings

Chocolate Swirl:

2 tablespoons granulated sugar

1/4 cup light corn syrup

3 tablespoons water

1 1/2 tablespoons prepared espresso coffee

1/4 cup plus 2 tablespoons cocoa powder

4 ounces bittersweet chocolate, chopped

1 1/2 tablespoons brandy

Pudding:

2 1/2 tablespoons water

1 1/2 tablespoons prepared espresso coffee

1/4 cup buttermilk

1/4 cup cocoa powder

3 ounces bittersweet chocolate, chopped

1/4 cup sour cream

1/2 cup butter, softened

1/4 cup plus 1 tablespoon firmly packed brown sugar

3 ounces almond paste

4 egg yolks

1 cup dried sour cherries, plumped in brandy **

1 1/4 teaspoons baking soda

1 tablespoon hot water

1 cup plus 2 tablespoons all-purpose flour, sifted

4 egg whites

2 tablespoons granulated sugar

1/4 cup melted butter

Cocoa powder for dusting

Whipped cream for garnish

** Montmorency Dried Sour Cherries™ work well.

For Chocolate Swirl: In a small saucepan, combine the sugar, corn syrup, water, espresso, and cocoa powder. Bring to a boil over medium heat and boil for 1 1/2 minutes, stirring constantly. Remove from heat, add the chocolate and stir until melted. Stir in the brandy, transfer to a bowl, and set aside to cool.

For Pudding: In a small saucepan, combine the water, espresso, and buttermilk. Bring to a boil over medium heat and whisk in the cocoa powder until dissolved. Remove from heat and add the chocolate and whisk until melted. Stir in sour cream. Transfer to a bowl and set aside to cool.

Using an electric mixer, cream the butter. Beat in the brown sugar, almond paste, egg yolks, and the above chocolate mixture (chocolate mixture from the pudding directions). Add the drained cherries.

Dissolve the baking soda in hot water. Add half of the flour to the chocolate mixture and mix well. Stir in the baking soda mixture. Add the remaining flour and mix until incorporated.

In a separate bowl with clean beaters, beat the egg whites until soft peaks form. Gradually add the granulated sugar and beat until stiff shiny peaks form. Fold the beaten egg whites into the cooled pudding mixture.

Brush 11 6 ounce custard cups or 1 8-cup mold with melted butter. Dust with cocoa powder, tapping out any excess. You will need enough pots to steam molds in. Place a trivet or steamer rack in the bottom of the pots and fill with water several inches above the rack. Begin heating the water to boil.

Pour the chocolate swirl mixture over the pudding mixture and mix just enough to form large swirls throughout the batter. Transfer the batter, evenly into the molds, filling no more than 2/3 full. Cut small squares of aluminum foil and cover each mold tightly (or place lid on 8-cup mold). Place the molds into the pots, adding additional boiling water to bring the level halfway up the sides of the molds. Cover the pot and steam at a simmer for 20 minutes (the 8-cup mold will take about 90 minutes and may periodically need the water level replenished). The pudding is done when firm to the touch. Uncover and remove to a cooling rack for 15 minutes. Invert and tap out onto a serving plate. Serve immediately with whipped cream.

Recipe Tester's note: When completely cool, this dessert can be covered and stored in the refrigerator. Reheat for a few seconds in the microwave before serving.

> During the 17th and 18th centuries, chocolate was prescribed as a cure-all for many ailments, including typhoid fever.

Chocolate Crème Brulee in Chocolate Sour Cherry Brioche

Gourmet Magazine's readers' poll voted Diva at the Met as Vancouver, B.C.'s best restaurant. This dessert illustrates why.

Makes 6 servings

Dark Chocolate Crème Brulee:

1 cup whipping cream

6 1/2 tablespoons half and half

3 1/2 ounces chopped semi-sweet chocolate

2 eggs

3 egg yolks

6 tablespoons granulated sugar

Chocolate Sour Cherry Brioche:

1 1/2 tablespoons dry yeast

1/4 cup warm water

2 cups all-purpose flour, divided

3 tablespoons granulated sugar, plus extra for sprinkling

2 1/2 tablespoons unsweetened cocoa powder

1/4 teaspoon salt

1 extra-large egg

1/2 cup butter, softened

1/3 cup chopped sun-dried sour cherries (Montmorency™ cherries)

1 large egg, beaten with 1 tablespoon milk

Sour Cherry Port Compote:

1 cup Port wine

1/4 cup red wine

1 3/4 cups sun-dried sour cherries (Montmorency™ cherries)

2 tablespoons granulated sugar

Dash lemon juice

For Dark Chocolate Crème Brulee: Preheat oven to 300 degrees. Butter a 1-quart baking dish.

Place the cream and half and half in a saucepan and bring to a boil.

Place the chopped chocolate in a bowl and pour the boiling cream mixture over. Stir until chocolate is melted and mixture is combined.

In another bowl, whisk together the eggs, egg yolks, and sugar. Pour in a little of the chocolate mixture and mix well. Add the remaining chocolate mixture and stir to combine.

Pour into prepared dish and bake for about 1 hour or until set. Remove from oven and cool to room temperature. Refrigerate until needed for brioche.

For Chocolate Sour Cherry Brioche: Stir the yeast into the warm water and let stand for 5 minutes to dissolve.

Combine the dissolved yeast, 3 tablespoons flour and sugar in the bowl of an electric mixer. Stir with the dough hook to make a sponge (a batter-like dough).

Combine the remaining flour, cocoa powder, and salt and sift over the sponge. Do NOT stir the dry ingredients into the sponge. Let stand until the sponge "cracks" through the dry ingredients (until the sponge rises above the dry ingredients).

Add the eggs to the dry ingredients and mix with the dough hook until the dough is smooth and elastic and comes away from the sides of the bowl to form a ball.

Continue mixing while adding the butter, a little at a time. Mix until the dough is smooth and shiny and comes away from the sides of the bowl. Add the sour cherries and mix until just incorporated.

> The #1 selling candy bar in the United States is Snickers.

Place dough in a large bowl, cover with plastic wrap and let stand in a warm place until the dough doubles in size.

Punch down dough to expel gas. Return to the bowl, cover with plastic wrap and refrigerate overnight.

Roll dough to approximately 1/2-inch thickness. Cut with 3-inch round cookie cutter.

Brush the edges with the egg wash. Place a small scoop of crème brulee onto the center of each round. Gather the edges of the dough together and pinch to seal. Let stand in a warm place until doubled in size.

Preheat oven to 325 degrees.

Gently brush each brioche with egg wash, sprinkle with sugar, and bake for 15 to 20 minutes, or until done.

Serve warm with Sour Cherry Port Compote and Chocolate Fudge Ice Cream (see p. 162).

For Sour Cherry Port Compote: Combine the Port, red wine, and cherries and let stand for 30 minutes. Strain liquid and reserve.

Place the sugar in a small saucepan. Stir in 1 tablespoon water and cook over medium heat, without stirring, until the mixture becomes a rich amber color.

Carefully add the reserved wine. Cook, stirring occasionally, until the mixture is reduced by half. Stir in the cherries and lemon juice and bring to a boil. Remove from heat and store in an airtight container.

Espresso White Chocolate Mousse in Orange Almond Lace Cookie Baskets

While less talked about than some of Seattle's other restaurants, Kaspar's is one of this author's favorites. The entrees are a delight, but do leave room for their absolutely delectable desserts. This Espresso White Chocolate Mousse is like rich pillows of cream with a subtle espresso flavor. The thin almond basket adds a buttery, lacy crunch.

Makes 6 to 8 servings

Orange Almond Lace Cookie Baskets:
>   3/4 cup granulated sugar
>   1/2 cup almonds, chopped
>   6 tablespoons all-purpose flour
>   Juice and grated peel of 1/2 orange
>   1/3 cup melted unsalted butter

Mousse:
>   4 3/4 cups whipping cream, divided
>   3 cups white chocolate chips
>   2 tablespoons instant coffee powder
>   2 tablespoons hot brewed espresso or strong coffee

For Cookie Baskets: Preheat oven to 400 degrees. Line a baking sheet with parchment paper.

Combine the sugar, almonds, and flour in a large mixing bowl. Make a well in the center and add orange juice, orange peel, and melted butter. Mix with a wooden spoon until well combined.

Drop by heaping tablespoons down the middle of the baking sheet, leaving about 3 inches between each cookie. There should be only three cookies per sheet. Flatten each cookie with a fork dipped in cold water (to about 1/16 inch).

Bake for 5 to 7 minutes or until golden brown. Turn baking sheet halfway through baking time and check often to make sure they don't burn.

In 1876, milk chocolate was born when Daniel Peter of Switzerland added milk to chocolate. Later, Mr. Peter sold his process to Henri Nestlé, who created the world's largest chocolate company.

Remove from oven and allow to cool for one minute. Cookies should be firm but still flexible.

Working quickly, lift one cookie with a metal spatula and drape over an inverted coffee cup, creating a cookie basket.

Repeat with all cookies. Allow to cool completely while molded over coffee cups. Store in a dry place.

For Mousse: In a saucepan, bring 2 3/4 cups cream to a rapid boil. Remove from heat and whisk in white chocolate chips, stirring until completely melted. Chill in refrigerator for at least one hour.

Dissolve coffee powder in hot espresso and cool.

Whip the remaining 2 cups cream until stiff peaks form.

Stir together the white chocolate sauce and espresso. Fold in whipped cream until well combined.

Serve in an Orange Almond Lace Cookie Basket.

Gram's Chocolate Banana Bread Pud'n

This Chocolate Banana Bread Pud'n is warm, rich, and comforting. The recipe, however, has several steps and takes some time to make. If you're in a hurry, you can always purchase the banana bread and chocolate cake.

Makes 12 servings

Gram's Banana Bread:

1 3/4 cups all-purpose flour

3/4 teaspoon baking soda

1 1/2 teaspoons cream of tartar

1/2 teaspoon salt

1/3 cup vegetable shortening

2/3 cups granulated sugar

2 eggs

1 cup mashed ripe bananas (1 to 2 bananas)

Ellen's Chocolate Cake:

2/3 cup unsweetened cocoa powder

2 1/4 cups granulated sugar

2 cups boiling water

2/3 cup vegetable oil

3 eggs

2 teaspoon vanilla

1 1/3 cups cake flour

1 1/4 cups all-purpose flour

1/2 teaspoon salt

1 1/2 teaspoons baking soda

Custard for Bread Pud'n:

4 cups whipping cream

2 cups half and half

1 cinnamon stick

5 cardamom pods, crushed

1/4 teaspoon ground cinnamon

1 vanilla bean, split and seeds scraped

12 eggs

1 cup firmly packed brown sugar

3/4 cups granulated sugar

Rum Crème Anglaise:
- 2 cups whipping cream
- 1 teaspoon vanilla
- 5 tablespoons granulated sugar
- 5 egg yolks
- Dark rum to taste

Bittersweet Chocolate Sauce:
- 2 cups hot coffee
- 24 ounces chopped bittersweet chocolate
- 1/2 cup unsalted butter, room temperature
- 2 teaspoons ground cinnamon, optional
- 2/3 cup granulated sugar
- 1/3 cup firmly packed brown sugar

Caramelized Banana Slices: (optional)
- 3 ripe bananas
- Granulated sugar

For Gram's Banana Bread: Preheat oven to 350 degrees. Spray a 9 by 5-inch loaf pan with non-stick spray. Line the pan with parchment paper and spray again.

Sift together the flour, baking soda, cream of tartar, and salt. Set aside.

In the bowl of an electric mixer, cream the shortening and sugar until light and fluffy. Add eggs, one at a time, beating well after each addition.

Add the flour mixture and the mashed banana alternately to the creamed mixture, beginning and ending with flour. Stir just until the flour is incorporated.

Pour the batter into the prepared loaf pan. Bake for 45 to 60 minutes or until a toothpick inserted in the center comes out clean. Remove from oven and cool in pan for 10 minutes. Turn out onto a wire rack and cool completely.

> Chocolate contains calcium, iron, thiamine, riboflavin, niacin, and vitamin C.

For Ellen's Chocolate Cake: Preheat oven to 350 degrees. Spray a 10-inch cake pan with non-stick spray. Line the bottom of the pan with parchment paper. Spray again with non-stick spray.

Into the bowl of an electric mixer, sift the cocoa powder and sugar. Add the boiling water and mix with the whip attachment on low speed for 3 minutes.

In a medium bowl, whisk together the vegetable oil, eggs and vanilla. Add the egg mixture to the cocoa mixture and whip on high speed for 3 minutes.

Sift together the cake flour, all-purpose flour, salt, and baking soda. Add to the cocoa mixture and beat on high speed for another 3 minutes.

Pour the batter into the prepared pan and bake for about 1 hour and 15 minutes or until the edges begin to pull away from the sides of the pan. Check after 1 hour. Top may crack slightly, but this is not a problem. Allow to cool in pan for 10 minutes then turn out onto a wire rack and cool completely.

For Custard for Bread Pud'n: In a large stainless steel pan, bring the cream, half and half, cinnamon stick, cardamom pods, ground cinnamon, and vanilla bean to a boil. Remove from heat and allow to cool.

Whisk together the eggs, brown sugar, and granulated sugar until well combined. When cream mixture is cool, add the egg mixture and stir well. Strain through a fine mesh strainer.

Rum Crème Anglaise: In a heavy saucepan, heat the cream, vanilla, and 2 1/2 tablespoons sugar until tiny bubbles form around the edges. Let cool for 10 minutes.

> Chocolate mousse, a classic French dessert, was invented by the painter Henri de Toulouse-Lautrec. It was originally called "chocolate mayonnaise."

In a bowl, whisk together the egg yolks and remaining sugar. Stir half of the warm cream mixture into the egg mixture and then return the egg/cream mixture to the saucepan. Stir well. Cook over low heat, stirring constantly with a heatproof rubber spatula, until the sauce coats the back of a spoon.

Strain through a fine mesh strainer and cool by placing the bowl of sauce in a larger bowl of ice water. Stir in rum to taste (2 to 4 tablespoons will probably do). Refrigerate until ready to use.

For Bittersweet Chocolate Sauce: In the top of a double boiler, combine the coffee, chocolate, butter, cinnamon, and sugars. Heat over hot water, stirring constantly, until the mixture is melted and smooth. Cool to room temperature. Store in refrigerator and reheat in a double boiler as needed.

To Assemble Bread Pud'n: Preheat oven to 350 degrees. Butter a 9 by 13-inch baking dish.

Cut banana bread into 1/2-inch cubes. Cut chocolate cake into 1/2-inch cubes. Put cubes into a buttered casserole, alternating layers to create a "checkerboard" effect.

Pour cold Bread Pud'n custard over the cubes, trying to wet all the top cubes, until you can just see the custard coming up through the cubes (about halfway up in the pan). You may not use all of the custard.

Press down on the cubes to soak up all of the custard. Do this a couple of times to be sure the top layer of cubes are soaked thoroughly with the custard. Only add more custard if the top seems dry. Cover the pan with aluminum foil.

Place the covered pan into a larger pan and pour boiling water into the larger pan until the water comes halfway up the side of the pud'n pan.

Bake for 1 to 2 hours. Check after 1 hour, and often thereafter. When pud'n is firm to the touch and no longer soupy, uncover and carefully remove from hot water bath. Continue baking for 10 to 15 minutes or until the top is a little crunchy.

Remove from oven and cool on wire rack for 15 to 20 minutes.

For Caramelized Banana Slices: Slice bananas into 1/4-inch slices on the bias (45 degree angle). Place on a baking sheet. Sprinkle each slice with granulated sugar to coat. Place pan under the broiler and broil until sugar melts and caramelizes (watch carefully).

To Serve: Place a small ladle of Rum Crème Anglaise (about 1/4 cup) in the bottom of a dessert bowl. Place a warm bread pudding portion in the pool of sauce. Drizzle with warm chocolate sauce. Top with a generous dollop of whipped cream. Garnish with Caramelized Banana Slices, if desired.

White Chocolate Bread Pudding with Bourbon Sauce

*We'd gathered 100 recipes for **The Chocolate Lover's Guide Cookbook** and were close to going to press when I realized we didn't have the recipe for this extraordinary White Chocolate Bread Pudding from 3 Doors Down. Stop the presses! I rushed over to this tiny neighborhood eatery and begged owner/chef Dave Marsh give us recipe #101. It was worth it.*

Makes 6-8 servings

For the Bread Pudding:

16 cups French bread (or about 1 1/2 1-pound baguettes),
    cut into 1 1/2-inch cubes
6 ounces white chocolate, chopped
2 cups milk
1 1/3 cups cream
6 tablespoons unsalted butter
2/3 teaspoon almond extract
2 teaspoons vanilla
2 egg yolks
2 eggs
1/3 cup + 1 tablespoon raisins, separated
1/2 cup sugar
fresh nutmeg to taste

For the Bourbon Sauce:

1 cup sugar
1/2 cup bourbon
4 tablespoons unsalted butter
2 tablespoons cream
1 egg yolk

For the Bread Pudding: Preheat oven to 350 degrees. Butter a 4-quart casserole.

Heat milk, cream, white chocolate, butter, almond extract, and vanilla over medium heat until mixture comes to a simmer and chocolate and butter are melted. Do not boil.

Soak raisins in a little bourbon for a few minutes to plump. Drain. Then add 1/3 cup raisins to cream mixture. Reserve 1 tablespoon raisins.

In a bowl, cream sugar and eggs together. Add cream-chocolate mixture and mix until well-incorporated.

Place one layer of bread cubes into pan and soak with half of the cream mixture. Be sure all pieces are well-soaked. Add the remaining bread cubes and soak with the remaining cream mixture. Top with 1 tablespoon raisins and fresh grated nutmeg.

Cover with foil and place pan into a larger pan. Fill the larger pan with hot water until it is at least halfway up the sides of the pudding pan. Bake at 350 degrees for 45-55 minutes or until set. The pudding is done when you press the pudding and no liquid rises to the top.

Serve warm with Bourbon Sauce.

Recipe Tester's note: If you like the top crispy (we do!), remove the foil during the last 10 minutes of baking.

For the Bourbon Sauce:

In a saucepan, heat sugar and bourbon over medium heat until the sugar is dissolved and the mixture is completely clear. Whisk in butter and cream. In a small bowl, beat egg yolk and add a tablespoon of the hot syrup mixture to the egg. Then add the egg to the sugar mixture and beat until all ingredients are smooth. Spoon the warm sauce over individual servings of bread pudding.

> Spanish ladies were so fond of chocolate, they had servants bring it to them during church services. The custom didn't please church officials.

Recipe Tester's note: The Bread Pudding and Bourbon Sauce can be covered and refrigerated. Reheat to warm in the microwave (20-30 seconds per serving).

Red Star Tavern and Roast House, Portland, Oregon

Earl Grey Tea and Chocolate Custard

Another offering from Red Star Roast House, the Earl Grey Tea and Chocolate Custard, is easy to make and has a silky texture chocolate lovers will enjoy.

Makes 8 servings

> 3 cups whole milk
> 1 cup whipping cream
> 3 Earl Grey tea bags (strings tied together)
> 12 ounces chopped bittersweet chocolate
> 4 eggs
> 6 egg yolks
> 1/2 cup plus 1 1/2 tablespoons granulated sugar
> 1 tablespoon vanilla
> 1/2 teaspoon salt

In a 2-quart stainless steel saucepan, combine the milk, cream, and tea bags. Heat over low heat until a skin forms on the top of the milk. Turn off the heat and allow the tea to steep for 10 minutes. Remove bags and squeeze out liquid and discard.

Add the chopped chocolate to the warm milk mixture and stir until melted and smooth.

Whisk together the eggs, egg yolks, sugar, vanilla, and salt. Add about half of the warm chocolate mixture to the egg mixture and stir well. Return the egg mixture to the chocolate mixture in the pan and stir well.

Strain through a fine mesh strainer into a stainless bowl. Chill by setting the bowl into another bowl of ice water. Cover and refrigerate the cooled custard base.

Preheat oven to 325 degrees.

Pour custard base into baking dishes or ovenproof teacups, leaving 1/4-inch space at top. Place the cups in a baking pan. Pour boiling water into the baking pan until it comes halfway up the sides of the cups.

Bake for 45 to 60 minutes or until the custard is set. The custard will only jiggle slightly when tapped.

"I am convinced that there is no such thing as a chocoholic. The very name offends me. The person who thinks he or she is, indeed, a chocoholic could in a different set of life circumstances be a pizzaholic, chain smoker, or compulsive turkey on rye with Russian dressing eater."

— Lora Brody, The Chocolate Diet

Ice Cream
& Sorbet

*With ice cream comes images of
carefree summer days. Treat yourself
and your guests to a bit of summer
anytime with homemade
ice creams and sorbets.*

Vanilla and Vanilla Mint
Ice Cream

At Duck Soup Inn, they make some of the lightest, most refreshing ice creams. They serve their Vanilla and Vanilla Mint Ice Creams with a Peppermint Brownie (see page 108). The wonderful ice creams can also be a dessert by themselves.

Makes 8 servings

> 2 eggs
> 2 tablespoons nonfat dry milk
> 1 cup granulated sugar
> 3 cups whipping cream
> 1 1/2 teaspoons vanilla
> 1 teaspoon peppermint extract (optional)

Blend eggs, dry milk, and sugar in a blender. Add the cream and vanilla and peppermint extract if using. Scrape the sides of the blender and blend until combined. Do not over blend. Freeze in an electric ice cream freezer according to manufacturer's directions.

Note: See raw egg caution, page 18.

Did you know that the Aztec emperor, Montezuma, actually invented ice cream? During the 16th century, he reportedly took snow from the top of a volcano and poured whipped, frothy "chocolatl" over it. It was the first chocolate ice cream!

Belgium Bittersweet Chocolate Ice Cream

Many people drive to Bow, Washington, to the Rhododendron Café just to enjoy chef Don Shank's incredibly rich and smooth Belgium Bittersweet Chocolate Ice Cream. Once you taste it, you'll know why.

Makes 1 gallon

> 1 1/3 cups half and half
> 2/3 cup whipping cream
> 1/4 cup coffee
> 7 tablespoons granulated sugar, divided
> 2 tablespoons plus 2 teaspoons butter
> 8 ounces Belgium bittersweet chocolate, broken into small pieces
> 4 egg yolks

Combine the half and half and cream in a small saucepan. Heat over medium heat until tiny bubbles form around the edge of the pan.

Make a simple syrup by combining the coffee and 3 1/2 tablespoons sugar in a small pan and simmering over medium heat for a few minutes. When syrup is ready, stir in the butter and chocolate and melt over low heat.

While whisking constantly, pour the scalded cream into the melted chocolate mixture until well combined.

In a large bowl, whisk together the remaining 3 1/2 tablespoons sugar and the egg yolks. Slowly whisk the hot chocolate mixture into the yolk-sugar mixture. Refrigerate until chilled. Pour into ice cream freezer and freeze according to manufacturer's directions.

Note: See raw egg caution, page 18.

Il Giardino di Umberto, Vancouver, B.C.
Chocolate Sorbet

This author used to think Chocolate Sorbet couldn't compare with ice cream. That's until I tried this rich, easy-to-make sorbet from Il Giardino di Umberto.

Makes about 6 cups

> 1/2 pound couverture chocolate, chopped (see page 200)
> 2 cups water
> 1/2 cup granulated sugar
> 1 vanilla bean, split lengthwise

Combine the chocolate, water, sugar, and vanilla bean in the top of a double boiler. Place over hot water and heat, stirring constantly, until chocolate is melted and mixture is combined. Cool.

Pour cooled mixture into the container of an ice cream freezer and freeze according to manufacturer's directions.

> Early Aztec Indians believed that drinking the chocolate beverage "chocolatl" brought them universal wisdom and knowledge.

The William Tell Restaurant (Georgian Court Hotel), Vancouver, B.C.

Chocolate Cinnamon Ice Cream

There's nothing quite like the combination of cinnamon and chocolate. This is a rich ice cream that doesn't cling to the palate.

Makes 1 gallon ice cream

> 2 cups 2 percent milk
> 7 ounces dark chocolate, chopped
> 4 eggs
> 1 1/3 cups granulated sugar
> 3 cups whipping cream
> 1 teaspoon ground cinnamon
> 1 vanilla bean split lengthwise

In a medium saucepan, scald milk by heating until tiny bubbles form around the edges of the pan. Add chocolate and stir until smooth.

In a large bowl, whisk the eggs until combined. Add the sugar, cream, and cinnamon and stir well. Scrape the vanilla seeds out of the split bean and add to the egg mixture, stirring well. Stir in the chocolate mixture. Refrigerate for 15 minutes.

Pour mixture into container of ice cream freezer and freeze according to manufacturer's directions. Transfer frozen ice cream to plastic containers and freeze overnight before serving.

Note: See raw egg caution, page 18.

Diva at the Met (Metropolitan Hotel), Vancouver, B.C.

Chocolate Fudge Ice Cream

This delightfully rich ice cream is served as a "side" to other desserts like Diva at the Met's Chocolate Créme Brulee in Chocolate Sour Cherry Brioche (see page 144). It's so good, it deserves to be enjoyed by itself.

Makes 6 servings

Ganache:
> 3/4 cup plus 2 tablespoons whipping cream
> 7 ounces chopped semi-sweet chocolate

Ice Cream Custard:
> 2 cups half and half
> 2 cups whipping cream
> 2 1/2 ounces chopped semi-sweet chocolate
> 8 egg yolks
> 1 cup granulated sugar

For ganache: Bring the cream to a boil in a small saucepan. Pour the boiling cream over the chopped chocolate and stir until the chocolate is melted and the mixture is smooth. Set aside.

For ice cream custard: Combine the half and half and the cream and bring to a boil. Pour over the chopped chocolate and stir until smooth.

Whisk together the egg yolks and the sugar. Pour a little of the hot cream mixture over the egg yolks and whisk to combine. Return the egg yolk and cream mixture to the hot cream mixture and stir to blend well. Return the mixture to the saucepan and cook, stirring constantly, until the cream is almost boiling. Do not boil.

Pour into a shallow pan and place over ice water to cool rapidly.

When mixture is cool, pour into the container of an ice cream freezer and freeze according to the manufacturer's directions. When the ice cream is just about done churning, open the container and gently stir in the chocolate ganache in a swirl pattern. Finish churning. Freeze for several hours to ripen.

> Swedish naturalist Carolus Linneaus renamed the term cocoa, "Theobroma Cocoa," Greek for "food of the Gods."

Paley's Place, Portland, Oregon

Caramel Ice Cream

This ice cream has a wonderfully rich caramel flavor. At Paley's Place, they serve it with a Hot Pecan Brownie (see page 111).

Makes 1 gallon

> 5 2/3 cups granulated sugar, divided
> 1 1/2 cups water
> 8 cups half and half
> 20 egg yolks
> 4 cups whipping cream

For Caramel Ice Cream: In a heavy-bottomed saucepan, heat 4 3/4 cups sugar over medium heat. Without stirring, continue to heat until the sugar is melted and has turned a rich brown color. (Watch as it turns quickly.)

Carefully add the water to the caramel mixture, stirring until smooth. Cool slightly.

Add the half and half to the caramel mixture and heat until very hot but not simmering.

Whisk the egg yolks with the remaining 14 tablespoons sugar until light and smooth.

Slowly whisk a small amount of the hot caramel mixture into the egg yolks and return to the saucepan. Cook until mixture reaches 178 degrees on a candy thermometer. Immediately strain into a container (to remove any cooked egg). Chill.

Whisk the whipping cream into the chilled custard and pour into the container of an electric ice cream freezer and freeze according to manufacturer's directions.

Cinnamon Ice Cream with Poached Pear and Dried Fruit Compote

At Seattle's Campagne restaurant, they serve their Warm Chocolate Torte (see page 59) with this Cinnamon Ice Cream with Poached Pear and Dried Fruit Compote. The ice cream has a lovely orange-cinnamon flavor that makes it a great dessert all by itself.

Makes 8 servings

Cinnamon Ice Cream:

2 cups whole milk

1 cup granulated sugar

1 1/2 teaspoons ground cinnamon

Zest of 1 orange

6 egg yolks

2 cups whipping cream

Poached Pear and Dried Fruit Compote:

3 cups water

1 1/2 cups granulated sugar

1/2 cup fresh lemon juice

1 vanilla bean, split lengthwise and scraped

1 cinnamon stick

Pinch whole allspice

Zest of 1 orange

1 bay leaf

2 teaspoons vanilla extract

4 firm Bosc pears, quartered and cored

1 1/2 cups dried fruit of your choice (black currants, diced apricots, dried cherries, dried cranberries, golden raisins etc.)

For Cinnamon Ice Cream: In a heavy-bottomed saucepan, heat milk, sugar, cinnamon, and orange zest until scalded, whisking occasionally to incorporate ingredients. Mixture is scalded when tiny bubbles form around the edges of the pan. Do not boil.

Whisk together the egg yolks. Ladle a small amount of the scalded milk into the yolks and whisk thoroughly. Whisk the egg mixture back into the saucepan. Using a rubber spatula, stir the mixture over low heat, using a figure 8 motion with the spatula. When the crème anglaise is done it will coat the spatula with a fine film. Do not boil!

Remove immediately from heat and strain into a plastic bowl or container. Whisk in the cream. Place mixture into a bowl of ice and stir occasionally until completely cool. Pour into container of ice cream freezer and freeze according to manufacturer's directions.

For Poached Pears and Dried Fruit Compote: In a medium sized, non-corrosive saucepan, mix the water, sugar, lemon juice, scraped vanilla seeds, cinnamon stick, allspice, orange zest, bay leaf, and vanilla extract. Whisk together over low heat until sugar is dissolved. Add pears and cook, covered, over low heat, stirring occasionally, until pears are translucent but still firm. Remove pears with slotted spoon and allow to cool.

Strain spices and zest from poaching liquid and return liquid to saucepan. Cook liquid over medium heat until reduced in volume by one-third. Add dried fruits and cool until they plump and soften. Allow mixture to cool.

Dice pears into small cubes and stir into dried fruit mixture. Compote can be served warm or chilled.

Note: See raw egg caution, page 18.

> The explorer Cortez planted cacoa trees wherever he explored. Thanks to him, cacao trees are found throughout Central America and Africa.

Bella Union Restaurant, Jacksonville, Oregon

Mud Pie

Because this uses ready-made ice cream, this is an easy recipe to make. You can change the ice cream flavor to your favorite.

Makes 12 servings

> 3 cups chocolate cookie crumbs
> 2 tablespoons granulated sugar
> 4 to 6 tablespoons melted butter
> 1 gallon Espresso Fudge Swirl ice cream
> 1 pound semi-sweet chocolate, chopped
> 3/4 cup whipping cream
> 1 1/2 cups whipped cream, for garnish
> Shaved chocolate, for garnish

Preheat oven to 350 degrees.

Combine the cookie crumbs, sugar, and melted butter in a bowl and mix well. Press evenly onto the bottom and up the sides of a 10-inch springform pan. Bake for 5 to 10 minutes or until set. Cool completely before filling.

Soften the ice cream until it is just workable. Press the softened ice cream into the cooled shell, making sure to press out any air pockets. Cover the top with plastic wrap and freeze immediately.

When ready to serve, place the chocolate and whipping cream in a heavy-bottomed saucepan and heat over low heat. Stir constantly until the chocolate is melted and mixture is completely smooth. Use immediately.

To serve, cut the pie into 12 pieces using a hot knife (re-dip knife in hot water between slices). Pour a pool of hot fudge sauce onto each serving plate and place a piece of pie on top. Garnish with whipped cream and chocolate shavings.

Recipe Tester's note: For an easy way to serve a large crowd, pour the hot fudge sauce over the entire mud pie and return to freezer until cool. To remove easily from pan, dip bottom and sides briefly in hot water.

Duck Soup Inn, Friday Harbor, Washington

Hot Fudge Sauce

This is one of the easiest and best hot fudge sauce recipes you'll find.

Makes 2 1/2 cups

> 1 cup whipping cream
> 1 cup granulated sugar
> 9 ounces Callebaut semi-sweet chocolate, chopped

Combine the cream and sugar in the top of a double boiler over medium heat. Heat, stirring, until the sugar is completely dissolved.

Remove double boiler from heat and stir in chopped chocolate. Allow to stand for about 10 minutes and then stir until chocolate is melted and sauce is completely smooth. Serve hot over ice cream.

> Songstress Barbara Streisand's favorite snack is reportedly coffee ice cream with chocolate fudge sauce.

Specialty Chocolate Desserts

A romantic evening with a loved one.
Important guests coming for dinner.
A celebration or festive holiday.
All of these deserve a specialty
chocolate dessert.

Bacchus Restaurant (Wedgewood Hotel), Vancouver, B.C.

Ravioli De Banana

This unusual dessert features crispy "ravioli" filled with warm chocolate and banana chunks.

Makes 8 servings

1/2 cup whipping cream
4 ounces chopped semi-sweet chocolate
2 eggs
2 teaspoons milk
1 large, ripe banana
1 package wonton wrappers
Vegetable oil for deep frying
Powdered sugar for garnish

In a small saucepan, bring the cream to a boil. Pour over chopped chocolate and whisk until chocolate is melted and smooth. Set chocolate mixture in refrigerator until slightly thickened.

Mix together the eggs and milk to make an egg wash. Peel and slice bananas 1/4-inch thick.

On a clean, dry surface lay out the wonton wrappers and brush tops with egg wash. Place a small teaspoonful of chocolate on half of the wonton wrappers. Top chocolate with a slice of banana. Top with the remaining wonton wrappers, pressing to remove air from ravioli. If you want round shaped ravioli instead of square, cut each with a round cookie cutter. Freeze ravioli until ready to use.

Heat oil in deep fryer to 350 degrees. Deep fry ravioli a few at a time until golden brown. Drain on paper toweling and dust with powdered sugar. Serve warm with ice cream of your choice.

Recipe Tester's note: If you don't have a deep fryer, use a deep pan and heat oil to 375 degrees. Fry one side golden brown, then turn and fry the other side. Remove with a slotted spoon and drain on paper towels. This recipe yields 24 won ton wrapper raviolis.

During the Gulf War, Hershey Foods developed the Dessert Bar, a chocolate bar that can withstand 140 degrees without melting.

Chocolate and Mascarpone Semifreddo with Kahlua Sauce

This chocolate and mascarpone cheese dessert is cool, light, and creamy.

Makes 10 servings

Semifreddo:

1 cup whipping cream
5 ounces chopped bittersweet chocolate
1 1/2 cups granulated sugar
1/4 cup water
7 egg yolks
1 cup mascarpone cheese (room temperature)
1 tablespoon Kahlua liqueur

Kahlua Sauce:

1 cup whipping cream
5 ounces finely chopped chocolate
2 tablespoons Kahlua

For Semifreddo: Whip the cream to medium peaks and set aside.

Place the chocolate in the top of a double boiler and set over hot water until melted, stirring occasionally. Set aside.

Put sugar and water in a saucepan and heat to 240 degrees on a candy thermometer.

Place the egg yolks in the bowl of an electric mixer and stir gently.

When sugar reaches 240 degrees, turn the mixer onto medium-high speed and slowly add sugar syrup to yolks. Turn mixer to high speed and beat until thick and pale (almost white). Reduce mixer speed to medium and continue mixing until yolk mixture is room temperature.

Add chocolate and beat until combined. Add mascarpone cheese and mix until just combined. Do not over mix or the cheese will separate. Stir in Kahlua.

Fold whipped cream into chocolate mixture and divide into containers and freeze for at least 6 hours.

For Kahlua Sauce: Place cream in a small saucepan and heat over medium heat until tiny bubbles form around the sides of the pan. Pour the scalded cream into the chopped chocolate and whisk until smooth. Stir in Kahlua and strain sauce. Keep warm but not hot.

To Serve: Scoop frozen semifreddo into serving bowls and drizzle warm Kahlua Sauce over top.

Note: See raw egg caution, page 18.

London Grill (Benson Hotel), Portland, Oregon
Chocolate Triangle

This elegant dessert takes a bit of effort, but the rich blending of the three chocolates is worth it.

Makes 12 servings

White Chocolate Layer:
6 ounces chopped white chocolate
1 cup plus 2 tablespoons whipping cream, divided

Milk Chocolate Layer:
14 ounces chopped milk chocolate
2 1/4 cups plus 2 tablespoons whipping cream, divided

Dark Chocolate Layer:
6 ounces chopped bittersweet chocolate
1 teaspoon mocha paste (see Chef's note)
1 1/4 cups whipping cream, divided

Line a triangular mold (24 inches long and 4 inches wide at the base) with plastic wrap.

For White Chocolate Layer: Place the white chocolate and 6 tablespoons whipping cream in the top of a double boiler. Melt chocolate over hot water, stirring until smooth. Cool.

Whip the remaining 3/4 cup cream until medium peaks form. Fold the whipped cream into the white chocolate mixture.

Using a pastry bag, fill the bottom of the mold with white chocolate mixture. Allow this layer to solidify before adding the next layer.

For Milk Chocolate Layer: Place the milk chocolate and 3/4 cup plus 2 tablespoons whipping cream in the top of a double boiler. Melt over hot water, stirring until smooth. Cool.

Whip the remaining 1 1/2 cups cream until medium peaks form. Fold the whipped cream into the milk chocolate mixture.

Using a pastry bag, fill this mixture almost to the top of the mold. This mixture is very soupy. Refrigerate until firm before adding the next layer.

For Dark Chocolate Layer: Place the bittersweet chocolate, mocha paste, and 1/2 cup whipping cream in the top of a double boiler. Melt over hot water, stirring until smooth. Cool.

Whip the remaining 3/4 cup cream until medium peaks form. Fold the whipped cream into the dark chocolate mixture.

Using a pastry bag fitted with a #8 plain tip, pipe the dark chocolate mixture over the top of the mold to cover completely. Refrigerate the mold until well chilled and the chocolate mixture is firm.

To serve, unmold the triangle onto a clean surface and remove plastic wrap. Slice individual servings with a clean hot knife.

Chef's note: Mocha paste is a form of concentrated coffee. It's available in better specialty stores or by mail order. Or you can make your own with a bit of espresso powder and enough water to make a paste.

> Archeologists believe Mayan Indians of Central America cultivated cacao trees (the source of cacao or chocolate beans) as early as the 7th century.

Pazzo Ristorante (Hotel Vintage Plaza), Portland, Oregon

Semifreddo alla Gianduja

This double-layer, semi-frozen dessert from pastry chef Diana Vineyard Copeland features the perfect blending of hazelnut and dark chocolate flavors with a cool, ultra-silky texture.

Makes 16 servings

Base:

8 ounces bittersweet chocolate

1/4 cup brewed espresso coffee

1/2 teaspoon hazelnut liqueur

8 egg yolks

1 1/2 cups powdered sugar

3/4 cup hazelnut flour (see Chef's note)

8 egg whites

1/4 cup granulated sugar

1 cup whipping cream

Mousse:

18 ounces bittersweet chocolate

3 tablespoons butter

1/2 cup whipping cream

5 ounces hazelnut paste

3/4 cup water

1 cup granulated sugar

3/4 cup egg whites (about 6 whites)

1 cup whipping cream

1/4 cup sour cream

For Base: Preheat oven to 350 degrees. Butter a 10-inch springform pan and wrap the outside, bottom, and sides with aluminum foil.

In the top of a double boiler over hot water, melt the chocolate. Set aside to cool slightly.

Combine the espresso and hazelnut liqueur in a small saucepan and heat.

In a large bowl of an electric mixer, whip egg yolks and powdered sugar until doubled in volume. Add hot espresso mixture and whip into yolk mixture. Stir in hazelnut flour. Fold egg yolk mixture into melted chocolate.

In a clean bowl of an electric mixer, whip the egg whites until foamy. Add the sugar and whip until stiff peaks form. Fold whipped whites into the chocolate mixture.

In another bowl from an electric mixer, whip the cream until soft peaks form. Fold into the chocolate mixture.

Pour mixture into prepared pan. Place springform pan into a larger pan and pour boiling water into the larger pan until it reaches half way up the sides of the springform pan. Cover with foil or a baking sheet and bake for 1 hour or just until set. Cool completely.

For Mousse: In the top of a double boiler, over hot water, melt chocolate, butter, and cream together. Set aside to cool slightly. Add hazelnut paste to chocolate but do not stir.

Dissolve sugar in water in a small saucepan. Bring to a boil over high heat. Remove from heat and transfer to a clean bowl. Cool for about 1 minute.

While syrup is cooling, whip the egg whites until soft peaks form. With mixer on medium speed, add the hot syrup in a slow steady stream. When all syrup has been added increase mixer speed to high and whip egg whites until mixture is cool (feel the bottom of the bowl).

Fold the hazelnut paste into the chocolate. Fold the egg whites into the chocolate in three additions.

Whip the cream with the sour cream until soft peaks form. Fold into the chocolate mixture.

Working quickly now, because as it cools it will stiffen up, pour the mousse onto the cooled base. Shake pan to level mousse. Cover with foil and freeze at least 8 hours or overnight.

Cut into 16 wedges using a hot dry knife.

Chef's note: The Semifreddo can be make in one day or you can make the base one day, the mousse the next.

To make 3/4 cup hazelnut flour, toast and skin 1/2 cup hazelnuts and grind in food processor into a fine powder. Mix with a scant 1/4 cup all-purpose flour.

> Steel is "tempered," cooled, reheated, and cooled, to make it stronger. Chocolate is tempered, too, to make it less likely to melt on store shelves and to give it a shiny look.

Chocolate Medallions

If you're in Spokane, Washington, stop at Windows of the Seasons and try this delightful dessert. Or take the challenge, and make it yourself. It starts with a thin medallion of chocolate cake that's topped with dark chocolate mousse, raspberries, and macaroons, all encased in a thin shell of dark chocolate.

Makes 10 servings

Chocolate Cake:
1/2 cup margarine or butter

2/3 cup granulated sugar

3 eggs, separated

4 ounces melted bittersweet chocolate

1 cup pastry flour

1/2 teaspoon baking powder

Macaroon:
1 1/2 ounce almond paste

1/2 cup granulated sugar

1 egg white

3/4 teaspoon rice flour

Chocolate Mousse:
2 ounces milk chocolate

10 ounces bittersweet chocolate

8 egg yolks, room temperature

3 cups whipping cream

Chocolate Strips:
Parchment paper, cut into ten 2 by 8 1/2-inch strips

4 ounces melted chocolate

Assembly:
10 tablespoons Framboise (raspberry liqueur)

1 cup fresh raspberries

Shaved chocolate for garnish

Powdered sugar for garnish

Raspberry coulis for garnish

For Chocolate Cake: Preheat oven to 350 degrees. Line a 12 by 17-inch rimmed cookie sheet with parchment paper. Grease the parchment and set aside.

In a large bowl with an electric mixer, cream the margarine and sugar until light and fluffy. Gradually add the 3 egg yolks to the creamed mixture. Stir in the melted chocolate.

Sift together the flour and baking powder. Fold flour mixture into the creamed mixture.

In medium bowl with an electric mixer, whip egg whites until soft peaks form. Gently fold the whipped egg whites into the chocolate mixture. Spread batter onto prepared baking sheet.

Bake for 12 to 15 minutes or until the cake tests done. Cool. Turn cake out of pan and remove parchment paper. Cut into discs using a 2 to 2 1/2-inch biscuit cutter. Set aside.

For Macaroons: Line a baking sheet with baker's parchment. Draw 10 circles on the parchment slightly smaller than the cake discs.

In a large bowl using an electric mixer, beat the almond paste until it is softened. Gradually add the sugar and mix until smooth. Beat in the egg white and rice flour.

With a pastry bag fitted with a plain tip, pipe the macaroon batter onto the circles that you drew on the parchment paper, filling each circle.

Bake at 350 degrees for about 15 to 20 minutes or until brown. Remove from parchment paper and cool on wire rack. If macaroons spread and are larger than the cake discs, use the biscuit cutter to cut down to size.

For Chocolate Mousse: Melt chocolate in the top of a double boiler over hot, not boiling, water, stirring frequently.

Warm a mixing bowl by filling with warm water. Let stand for 5 minutes, then empty bowl and wipe dry. Place yolks in bowl and whip until pale in color and triple in volume. Whisk in melted chocolate.

Place the cream in a chilled bowl and whip until stiff peaks form. Fold into chocolate mixture and refrigerate while assembling medallions.

For Assembly: Place chocolate cake discs on a flat surface. Quickly soak each macaroon in Framboise and place on top of cake. Place a few whole raspberries on top of the macaroon.

Dip one side of the parchment strips into the melted chocolate, holding onto the last 1/2-inch of paper. Let set for 2 to 3 minutes. Wrap the strip around the cake/macaroon discs with the paper on the outside. Place in the refrigerator to set for at least 30 minutes.

Once the chocolate has set, carefully remove the parchment strips. Fill the remaining space with chocolate mousse. Top with chocolate shavings and sprinkle with powdered sugar. Serve with a small amount of raspberry coulis.

Recipe Tester's notes: This complex recipe makes an attractive and tasty dessert. However, it requires many steps and advanced assembly skills. It should probably be attempted by only more advanced cooks.

Note: See raw egg caution, page 18.

Danish Cream Tosca

Pastry chef Wayne Kent's Danish Cream Tosca is a delight. It starts with buttery pastry with a thin layer of strawberry, followed by an almond praline center that's topped with toasted almonds. It's cut into triangles and the ends are dipped in dark chocolate.

Makes 30 servings

Tosca Dough:

- 3/4 cup plus 2 tablespoons unsalted butter
- 1 teaspoon vanilla
- 1 3/4 cups sifted powdered sugar
- 1 egg
- 2 1/4 cups all-purpose flour
- 1/2 teaspoon salt

Mazerine Filling:

- 1 pound 5 ounces almond paste
- 2 2/3 cups granulated sugar
- 1 cup eggs (about 9 eggs), divided
- 2 2/3 cups margarine or butter, softened
- 3/4 cup plus 2 tablespoons all-purpose flour

Almond Cream Topping:

- 4 tablespoons margarine
- 5 tablespoons butter
- 3/4 cup plus 1 tablespoon granulated sugar
- 4 1/2 tablespoons whipping cream
- 1/2 teaspoon vanilla
- 3 tablespoons light corn syrup
- 6 ounces sliced almonds

Assembly:

- 4 tablespoons strawberry jam
- 8 ounces melted chocolate

For Tosca Dough: In a mixer bowl, with a dough hook, mix butter, vanilla, sugar, and egg until well combined.

Stir together the flour and salt and add to the butter mixture. Mix until just smooth. Gather into a ball and wrap in plastic wrap. Refrigerate for about 30 minutes.

For Mazerine Filling: In a mixing bowl with a paddle attachment, break up the almond paste. Add the sugar and mix briefly. Gradually add 3/4 cup eggs and beat until smooth. Scrape bottom and sides of bowl occasionally.

Add margarine or butter and mix well, scraping bottom and sides of bowl occasionally. Add flour and beat well and then add remaining eggs. Mix to blend. Do not over mix.

For Almond Cream Topping: Combine the margarine, butter, sugar, cream, vanilla, and corn syrup in a medium saucepan. Heat over medium heat until the mixture simmers. Add almonds, stir well and remove from heat. Cool to warm before spreading on tosca dough.

For Assembly: Preheat oven to 350 degrees.

On a lightly floured surface, roll out tosca dough to a 13 by 18-inch rectangle. Fit onto the bottom and up the sides of an 11 1/2 by 16 1/2-inch baking sheet. Evenly puncture the bottom of the dough with fingertips. Spread a thin layer of strawberry jam over the bottom of the dough. Spread the mazerine filling evenly over the strawberry jam.

Bake for 45 minutes or until light brown and slightly springy to the touch. Let cool for 30 minutes.

Spread the almond cream topping over the top of the tosca and return to oven until the almonds turn a pale golden brown. Allow to cool until warm to the touch. Invert tosca onto the bottom of another baking pan and cover with waxed paper. Reinvert the tosca into the original baking pan. Cover and refrigerate overnight.

Slide the tosca out of the pan so that the almond cream is on top. Trim edges (they make an excellent snack) and cut tosca into desired shapes. Dip ends or edges into melted dark chocolate. Use your imagination and dip decoratively. Refrigerate until ready to serve or freeze if desired.

> To remove chocolate stains, use a bit of ammonia and water. It breaks down the oil base in the cocoa butter and lifts off the stain.

Pastazza, Bellingham, Washington
Chocolate Paté

This is Pastazza's signature dessert and it's a good one. This paté has an ultra-smooth texture and a wonderfully dark bittersweet flavor.

Makes 28-32 servings

> 30 ounces chopped bittersweet chocolate (we prefer Guittard)
> 8 tablespoons butter
> 2 cups whipping cream
> 8 egg yolks
> 1 cup granulated sugar
> 1 tablespoon vanilla (or other flavoring such as Kahlua or espresso)

In the top of a double boiler, over hot water (not boiling), melt the chocolate and butter, stirring often. While the chocolate is melting, heat the cream in a small saucepan, just until a skin forms on the top.

Beat egg yolks with the sugar until light and fluffy. Remove the chocolate from the heat and slowly stir in the egg yolk mixture in a thin stream. While stirring constantly, add the hot cream a little at a time.

Line the bottom and sides of an 8 1/2 by 4 1/2-inch loaf pan with plastic wrap. Pour the chocolate mixture into the pan and cool uncovered for an hour on a wire rack. Refrigerate for several hours or until completely chilled.

To serve, invert the loaf pan over a rectangular plate to unmold. Peel away the plastic wrap. Cut with a sharp, hot knife into 1/4-inch slices. Serve with raspberry sauce or créme anglaise.

Note: See raw egg caution, page 18.

> Montezuma always drank the chocolate drink, "chocolatl," before entering his harem. This was likely the beginning of the belief that chocolate is an aphrodisiac.

Chez Daniel, Victoria, B.C.

Chez Daniel's Classic Truffles

Award-winning Chef Daniel Rigollet says simple is best and, with this recipe, he proves his point. This is one of the easiest and most delicious truffle recipes you'll find. It keeps in the refrigerator for several weeks, ensuring you have a fabulous dessert for surprise company. It won a Best List Award from **The Chocolate Lover's Guide to the Pacific Northwest.**

Makes about 40 truffles

> 12 ounces chopped Callebaut chocolate
> 1 cup whipping cream
> 1/4 cup unsalted butter
> 2 tablespoons liqueur (your favorite flavor such as Kahlua,
>   Grand Marnier etc.), optional
> Unsweetened cocoa powder

In the top of a double boiler, over hot water, melt the chocolate.

While chocolate is melting, combine the cream and butter in a small saucepan and bring to a boil.

Combine the melted chocolate and boiling cream mixture in the bowl of an electric mixer. Beat on low speed for 7 to 8 minutes or until the mixture is cool. Beat in the liqueur.

Scrape into a bowl and cover. Refrigerate until needed.

Using a small scoop or teaspoon, scoop out small amounts of ganache and roll into balls. Roll in cocoa powder.

Chef's note: Roll in cocoa just before serving. Otherwise, the ganache absorbs some of the cocoa. For a bit of color, serve with a few pomegranate seeds.

Recipe Tester's note: This recipe lends itself to a variety of coatings, including chopped toasted almonds and hazelnuts, chopped white chocolate, and chopped coconut. Experiment and find the coatings you like the best.

La Petite Restaurant, Anacordes, Washington

Dutch Chocolate Roll

This Dutch Chocolate roll from La Petite Restaurant in Anacortes, Washington, features a delicate chocolate sponge cake that's filled with whipped cream and sliced jelly roll style. Easy to make, it's a melt-in-the-mouth creamy dessert sure to delight.

Makes 8 servings

> 9 ounces chopped bittersweet chocolate
> 6 tablespoons brewed espresso coffee
> 9 eggs, separated
> 1 cup granulated sugar (reserve 1 teaspoon)
> 1 teaspoon cream of tartar
> 1/4 cup Dutch process cocoa powder
> 1 cup whipping cream

Preheat oven to 375 degrees. Butter a 9 by 12-inch baking pan and line with waxed paper or parchment paper. Butter the waxed paper.

Combine the chocolate and espresso in a small saucepan. Heat over low heat, stirring constantly until chocolate is melted. Cool to room temperature, stirring occasionally.

In a large bowl, gently whisk the egg yolks while gradually adding the sugar. Set aside.

In a large clean bowl, whisk the egg whites with the 1 teaspoon sugar and cream of tartar until stiff but not dry. Stir the chocolate mixture into the egg yolks and then gently fold the chocolate mixture into the egg whites.

Spread the batter into the prepared pan and bake for 20 minutes. Cool to room temperature.

Dust cake with cocoa powder and gently brush off excess. Cover with waxed paper and then with a cutting board larger than the pan. Carefully invert the cake and remove the pan and waxed paper. If edges are crispy, trim off.

Whip cream until stiff peaks form. Spread whipped cream over cake and roll up, using the waxed paper as a guide. Refrigerate until ready to serve. Slice into 8 slices and serve.

Recipe Tester's note: Be sure the cake is completely cool before attempting to roll it.

> According to Mexican mythology, chocolate was the drink of choice of the gods in paradise. As a special blessing to man, the God of Air brought cacao seeds to earth.

Deli De Pasta, Yakima, Washington

Tiramisu

It's often difficult to find an excellent tiramisu, the classic Italian dessert. But if you've had a good one, you know how wonderful the blending of mascarpone, espresso, whipping cream, and ladyfingers can be. This recipe from Deli De Pasta in Yakima, Washington, won a Best List Award from **The Chocolate Lover's Guide to the Pacific Northwest** *and is one of the best this author has tasted.*

Makes 13 servings

> 1 1/2 pounds mascarpone cheese
> 1 cup powdered sugar
> 1 1/2 tablespoons plus 1/4 cup Kahlua liqueur, divided
> 2 cups whipping cream
> 1 teaspoon instant espresso powder
> 1/4 cup brewed espresso coffee, room temperature
> 1 1/2 to 2 boxes ladyfinger cookies
> Espresso powder in a shaker
> Unsweetened cocoa powder in a shaker
> Shaved chocolate for garnish

In a large bowl, mix together the mascarpone cheese, powdered sugar, and 1 1/2 tablespoons Kahlua.

In another bowl, whip the cream until stiff peaks form. Fold the whipped cream into the mascarpone cheese mixture. Chill.

In a small bowl, stir together the espresso powder, brewed espresso, and 1/4 cup Kahlua. Set aside.

Spray a 10-inch springform pan with nonstick cooking spray. Cut 39 ladyfingers to fit 1/2-inch above the rim of the springform pan. Liberally brush both sides of the ladyfingers with the espresso mixture and fit around the inside edge of the pan, sugar side out. Then brush the espresso mixture on the sugar side of enough ladyfingers to fit in the bottom of the springform pan.

Tightly fit the ladyfingers into the bottom of the pan, sugared side down. Sprinkle lightly with espresso powder. Sprinkle heavily with powdered cocoa.

Spread 1/2 of the mascarpone mixture over the ladyfingers. Brush the espresso mixture on enough ladyfingers to cover the mascarpone mixture. Lay ladyfingers over mascarpone mixture and top with remaining mascarpone mixture. Sprinkle with espresso powder and cocoa powder. Chill overnight. Cut with an electric knife into 13 wedges. Top with shaved chocolate.

Recipe Tester's note: The espresso mixture gives the ladyfingers their moisture. Be sure to use all the espresso when brushing the ladyfingers or the dessert will be dry.

Pazzo Ristorante (Hotel Vintage Plaza), Portland, Oregon
Tiramisu

This version of tiramisu uses rum instead of Kahlua. Like the Deli De Pasta recipe, Pazzo's version also won a Best List Award from **The Chocolate Lover's Guide to the Pacific Northwest.**

Makes 9 servings
Paint:
> 1 cup granulated sugar
>
> 3/4 cup brewed espresso coffee
>
> 1/4 cup dark rum

Filling:
> 1 1/2 cups whipping cream
>
> 3 teaspoon dark rum
>
> 1 teaspoon vanilla
>
> 1 pound mascarpone cheese
>
> 1 1/2 cups powdered sugar, sifted
>
> 1 1/2 to 2 boxes Ladyfingers
>
> Unsweetened cocoa powder

For Paint: Combine the sugar, espresso, and rum in a small saucepan and bring to a boil. Boil briefly until sugar is dissolved. Set aside to cool.

For Filling: In a large bowl, whip the cream with the rum and vanilla until soft peaks form.

In another large bowl, stir together the powdered sugar and mascarpone cheese. Fold in the whipped cream.

> Early Spanish nobility didn't like the bitterness of chocolate. They added honey and vanilla.

To Assemble: Arrange a single layer of ladyfingers in the bottom of an 8-inch square glass pan. Use a pastry brush to soak the ladyfingers with 1/3 of the paint.

Spread 1/3 of the mascarpone cheese over the ladyfingers. Sift a layer of cocoa over the mascarpone (using about 2 tablespoons). Repeat the layers two more times, finishing with a smooth layer of mascarpone cheese mixture. Reserve the final dusting of cocoa powder until just before serving.

Refrigerate for at least 1 hour or up to 24 hours. Cut into 9 squares, dust with cocoa powder and serve.

RiverPlace Hotel, Portland, Oregon

Triple Chocolate Terrine with Red and Black Raspberry Sauces

Anything that comes out of veteran pastry chef Colin Cameron's kitchen is going to be wonderful and his signature Triple Chocolate Terrine is no exception. It's a swirling combination of three silky mousses – white chocolate, milk chocolate, and dark chocolate.

Makes 8 servings

White Chocolate Mousse:
1/3 teaspoon unflavored gelatin
2/3 teaspoon cool water
2/3 teaspoon Triple Sec
4 ounces white chocolate
9 tablespoons whipping cream, divided
3 tablespoons crème fraiche **

Milk Chocolate Mousse:
9 ounces milk chocolate
1 1/4 cups whipping cream, divided
5 tablespoons plus 1 teaspoon crème fraiche **

Bittersweet Chocolate Mousse:
4 ounces bittersweet chocolate
2/3 teaspoon coffee extract
11 tablespoons whipping cream, divided
2 tablespoons plus 1 teaspoon crème fraiche **

Red Raspberry Sauce:
2 1/2 pints fresh red raspberries or 30 ounces frozen red raspberries
3/4 cup granulated sugar
1 1/2 tablespoons sifted cornstarch

Black Raspberry Sauce:
1 1/4 pints fresh black raspberries or 15 ounces frozen black raspberries
6 tablespoons granulated sugar
3/4 tablespoon sifted cornstarch

For White Chocolate Mousse: In a small bowl, whisk together the gelatin, water, and Triple Sec. Set aside.

In a double boiler, melt the white chocolate over hot, not boiling, water. Stir occasionally.

When chocolate is completely melted, scald 4 tablespoons whipping cream in a small saucepan. Remove from heat and stir in softened gelatin. Immediately stir cream and gelatin mixture into the melted chocolate, stirring rapidly until completely blended. Set aside to cool.

When cooled to room temperature, combine the remaining 5 tablespoons cream with 3 tablespoons crème fraiche and whip to soft peaks. Gently fold the whipped cream mixture into the cooled white chocolate mixture.

Prepare a clean 8 1/2 by 4 1/2-inch loaf pan by lining it with plastic wrap (a metal loaf pan works best for unmolding). Spoon White Chocolate Mousse into prepared pan, spread evenly, and refrigerate until set.

For Milk Chocolate Mousse: In a double boiler, melt the milk chocolate over hot, not boiling, water. Stir occasionally.

When chocolate is completely melted, scald 9 tablespoons whipping cream in a small saucepan. Immediately stir cream into the melted chocolate, stirring rapidly until completely blended. Set aside to cool.

When white chocolate mixture is cooled to room temperature, combine the remaining 11 tablespoons cream with 5 tablespoons and 1 teaspoon crème fraiche and whip to soft peaks. Gently fold the whipped cream mixture into the cooled milk chocolate mixture.

Spoon Milk Chocolate Mousse on top of the White Chocolate Mousse in the lined loaf pan, spreading smooth. Return the pan to the refrigerator to allow mousse to set.

For Bittersweet Chocolate Mousse: In a double boiler, melt the bittersweet chocolate with the coffee extract over hot, not boiling water. Stir occasionally.

When chocolate is completely melted, scald 6 tablespoons whipping cream in a small saucepan. Immediately stir cream into the melted chocolate, stirring rapidly until completely blended. Set aside to cool.

When cooled to room temperature, combine the remaining 5 tablespoons cream with 2 tablespoons and 1 teaspoon crème fraiche and whip to soft peaks. Gently fold the whipped cream mixture into the cooled bittersweet chocolate mixture.

Spoon Bittersweet Chocolate Mousse on top of the Milk Chocolate Mousse in the lined loaf pan, spreading smooth. Return the pan to the refrigerator to allow mousse to set. May also be frozen.

For Red Raspberry Sauce: If using frozen raspberries, thaw before proceeding.

Puree berries and strain through cheesecloth or wire strainer.

Combine the strained berries, sugar, and cornstarch in a saucepan. Stir until smooth and then cook over medium heat until sauce comes to a boil, stirring constantly. Boil for one minute and then remove from heat. Set aside to cool, stirring occasionally so the sauce doesn't form a skin. Refrigerate until needed.

For Black Raspberry Sauce: If using frozen berries, thaw before proceeding.

Purée berries and strain through cheesecloth or wire strainer.

Combine the strained berries, sugar, and cornstarch in a saucepan. Stir until smooth and then cook over medium heat until sauce comes to a boil, stirring constantly. Boil for one minute and then remove from heat. Set aside to cool, stirring occasionally so the sauce doesn't form a skin. Refrigerate until needed.

To Serve: Unmold terrine onto a cutting board by dipping the loaf pan in cool water, then inverting. Do not use hot water as this may slightly melt the mousse. If you have used a metal loaf pan, flex the bottom with your thumbs to pop out the terrine. If you've used a glass or ceramic loaf pan, you may need to hold the pan in the cool water longer. Peel off the plastic wrap.

Dip a sharp knife in hot water, wipe dry, then cut the terrine into 8 equal pieces, repeating the hot water procedure for each cut.

Place each slice cut side down on a serving plate.

Thin the sauces, if necessary, with a little water. The sauces should be just thin enough that they "flow" when placed onto the plate, without being runny. Ladle some Red Raspberry Sauce onto the plate next to each slice of terrine. Drizzle some of the Black Raspberry Sauce over the top of each slice, being careful not to cover the surface completely.

Chef's note: At the hotel, we make all three mousses at the same time, and swirl them together in the pan. The resulting effect is wonderful—done properly, each slice of the terrine looks a little bit different from all the other slices. I like to call this dessert my example of the mathematical principle of "chaos theory." There are random results (the different appearance of each slice) within very definite limits (the quantities of the mousse; this is why there's twice as much of the Milk Chocolate Mousse as the other two, so all three will appear to be equal amounts, though they aren't). It may be fun to experiment and swirl the mousses together a little as you deposit them in the loaf pan, or vary the order in which they're made.

** **Crème Fraiche** is like a mild version of sour cream. If you're pressed for time, you can substitute an equal amount of sour cream for crème fraiche in the mousses. However, the mousses will have a slightly sharper flavor to them. Or easily make your own crème fraiche.

> 1/2 cup whipping cream (not ultra-pasteurized cream)
> 1 teaspoon buttermilk (or yogurt or sour cream)

Start the crème fraiche at least two days before using it.

Stir the buttermilk into the whipping cream. Place in a warm place and allow to stand until it thickens to the consistency of yogurt or sour cream (8-24 hours). Refrigerate. Can be refrigerated for up to 10 days. It can be spooned over fresh fruit, warm cobblers, or used in sauces or soups (it can be boiled without curdling).

Marjolaine

While this recipe is lengthy, it isn't difficult, and the resulting soft and crunchy textures and chocolate, hazelnut, and praline flavors are heavenly. This version uses chocolate mousse instead of chocolate cream to top the dessert.

Makes 12 servings

Meringue:

1 cup hazelnuts
1 3/4 cups blanched sliced almonds
1 3/4 cups granulated sugar
2 tablespoons all-purpose flour
3 tablespoons melted butter
8 egg whites
A pinch of salt

Praline buttercream:

1 cup granulated sugar, divided
3/4 cup water
1/4 cup toasted hazelnuts
1/4 cup toasted almonds
3 egg yolks
1 cup unsalted butter, softened (2 sticks)
2 tablespoons brewed espresso coffee
2 tablespoons hazelnut liqueur

Chocolate mousse:

1 pound chopped semi-sweet chocolate
1/2 cup butter (1 stick)
11 egg yolks (1 cup)
12 egg whites

Crème Fraiche:

1 cup whipping cream
1 cup sour cream

Garnish:

Melted chocolate

For Meringue: Preheat oven to 400 degrees. Line two 12 by 17-inch rimmed baking sheets with parchment paper. Brush generously with melted butter. Set aside.

Place the hazelnuts and almonds on separated baking sheets. Roast almonds approximately 5 minutes and hazelnuts 10 to 12 minutes. Almonds should be golden brown. Transfer hazelnuts to a clean towel and rub with towel to remove skins.

Reserve 2 tablespoons sugar and combine the remaining sugar with the almonds and hazelnuts and flour in the bowl of a food processor. Process until nuts are finely ground and mixture resembles coarse meal. Set aside to cool.

Whip the egg whites and salt until soft peaks form. Add the reserved 2 tablespoons sugar and continue to beat until stiff peaks form. Fold in the cooled nut mixture.

Spread the meringue onto the two prepared baking sheets. The layers should be about 1/8 inch thick. Bake for 10 to 12 minutes or until golden brown. Remove from oven and allow to cool.

When cool enough to handle, turn layers onto a smooth surface and carefully remove parchment paper.

For Praline Buttercream: In a small saucepan, combine 3/4 cup of the sugar and 1/4 cup water and bring to a boil. Boil until the bubbles are clear and the syrup is thick. Add the nuts and continue cooking until the syrup is a dark caramel color and the nuts are brown. Add the remaining 1/2 cup water and cook 1 to 2 minutes longer to liquefy the caramel.

In an electric mixer, beat the egg yolks with the remaining 1/4 cup sugar until light and fluffy. Strain the hot caramel syrup into the egg yolks, reserving the nuts for another use. Continue beating until the mixture is cool.

Beat the butter into the cooled egg yolk mixture, 1 tablespoon at a time. When the butter is completely incorporated add the espresso and liqueur. Chill.

For Chocolate Mousse: In the top of a double boiler over hot water, melt the chocolate and butter. Whisk to combine. Combine the chocolate mixture and the egg yolks in the bowl of an electric mixer and beat until thick and cool.

In a clean bowl, beat the egg whites until stiff peaks form. Be careful not to over beat or the whites will be dry. Fold the chocolate mixture into the egg whites and chill for 12 hours or until set.

For Crème Fraiche: Combine the whipping cream and sour cream in a medium bowl and let stand, covered, at room temperature, overnight. Using an electric mixer, beat the cream until stiff peaks form. Set aside.

To Assemble: Cut each meringue in half lengthwise, making 4 rectangles. Reserve the smoothest layer for the top. Place the first layer on a serving plate and spread with chocolate mousse.

Top with second layer and spread with praline butter cream. Place third meringue layer on top of praline butter cream and spread with whipped crème fraiche. Place reserved meringue layer on top. Trim sides with a serrated knife, if necessary. Chill marjolaine.

To serve, drizzle melted chocolate over top in decorative pattern. Using a hot, dry serrated knife, cut into 12 servings.

Note: See raw egg caution, page 18.

Zefiro, Portland, Oregon

Chocolate Marjolaine

Zefiro's Chocolate Marjolaine features big slabs of hazelnut-studded meringue layered with rich, dark chocolate ganache.

Makes 10 servings

Meringue:

3/4 cup toasted hazelnuts

1 1/2 cups toasted unblanched almonds

1 tablespoon all-purpose flour

1 1/2 cup granulated sugar, divided

1 cup egg whites (about 8 whites)

Chocolate Ganache:

2 1/3 cups whipping cream

8 ounces finely chopped Callebaut semi-sweet chocolate or
other fine quality scmi-swcct chocolate

Chocolate Glaze:

8 ounces finely chopped Guittard bittersweet chocolate, or
other fine quality bittersweet chocolate

5 tablespoons butter

1/3 cup whipping cream

1/3 cup water

For Meringue: Preheat oven to 300 degrees. Line two 12 by 17-inch rimmed baking pans or jelly roll pans with parchment paper. Grease and flour the parchment.

Place the nuts, flour, and 1/2 cup sugar in the bowl of a food processor and grind until nuts are very fine. Remove to a large bowl.

Whip egg whites with an electric mixer until they are frothy. Continue whipping, gradually adding the remaining 1 cup sugar until whites hold stiff peaks. Fold whites into nut mixture.

Spread meringue onto the prepared pans. The layers should be about 1/4-inch thick.

Bake in preheated oven for about 40 minutes. Meringues are done when they are crisp through after cooling.

For Chocolate Ganache: Bring cream to a boil and turn off. Slowly pour hot cream over chopped chocolate while whisking constantly. Whisk until chocolate is completely melted and mixture is smooth. Strain and chill thoroughly.

For Chocolate Glaze: Combine chopped chocolate and butter in top of a double boiler. Place over hot, not boiling, water and melt slowly.

Combine cream and water and slowly whisk into melted chocolate mixture. Strain and cool until glaze reaches spreading consistency.

To Assemble: Carefully remove baked meringues from pans, leaving parchment paper intact. With a serrated knife, carefully cut meringue into 4 strips crosswise (see note below). Each strip should measure about 4 1/2 by 12-inches and have parchment paper intact underneath.

Dust surface where marjolaine is to be assembled with cocoa powder to prevent it from sticking.

Stir cooled ganache in mixer with paddle attachment until stiff enough to spread.

Begin layering marjolaine. Remove parchment paper from one strip of meringue. Place on cocoa dusted surface. Spread evenly with 1/2 cup ganache. Continue layering in this manner until you have used seven layers of meringue and six layers of ganache (ending with meringue). Chill in refrigerator for two hours.

When chilled, trim sides with serrated knife. Spread a thin layer of chocolate glaze over top and sides of marjolaine. Refrigerate until glaze hardens.

To serve, slice into 10 pieces with hot, dry serrated knife.

Chef's note: Don't worry if some of the meringue pieces break when they are cut. Pieces can be put back together like a jigsaw puzzle in between layers of ganache.

> Believing that chocolate lighted the fires of passion, Joan Franc Rauch of Vienna, in 1624, suggested that monks be banned from drinking chocolate.

Chocolate-Raspberry Bombes

These delightful bombes feature mocha cake and a milk chocolate raspberry mousse that's enrobed in dark chocolate.

Makes 8 servings

Crème Fraiche:

> 1/2 cup whipping cream (do not use ultra-pasteurized cream)
>
> 1 teaspoon buttermilk (or yogurt or sour cream)

Mocha Cake:

> 1 2/3 cups granulated sugar
>
> 1 1/2 cups unsifted all-purpose flour
>
> 3/4 cup Dutch process cocoa powder
>
> 1 teaspoon baking powder
>
> 1 teaspoon baking soda
>
> 1/2 cup plus 2 tablespoons whole milk, room temperature
>
> 1/2 cup plus 2 tablespoons strong coffee, room temperature
>
> 2 eggs
>
> 1 1/4 teaspoons vanilla

Chocolate-Raspberry Mousse:

> 10 1/2 ounces milk chocolate
>
> 1 3/4 cups whipping cream, divided
>
> 8 ounces fresh or frozen raspberries
>
> 1/2 cup crème fraiche (see above recipe)
>
> 8 4-ounce ramekins or aluminum foil cups
>
> 1 round cookie cutter of same size as ramekins

Chocolate Glaze and Decoration:

> 12 ounces bittersweet chocolate
>
> 12 tablespoons unsalted butter
>
> 2 or 3 ounces white or milk chocolate, melted

For Crème Fraiche: Start the crème fraiche at least two days before you plan to serve the bombes.

Stir the buttermilk into the whipping cream. Place in a warm place and allow to stand until it thickens to the consistency of yogurt or sour cream. Refrigerate.

For Mocha Cake: Preheat oven to 375 degrees. Grease the sides and bottom of a 12 by 18-inch rimmed baking pan or jelly-roll pan. Line the pan with parchment paper.

Sift the sugar, flour, cocoa powder, baking powder, and baking soda into a mixing bowl. Whisk together the milk, coffee, eggs, and vanilla and then stir into the dry ingredients until just combined. The batter will be fairly liquid.

Pour the batter into the prepared pan. Bake until the cake is set and springy in the center, about 7 to 8 minutes. The cake will be about 1/4-inch thick. Remove from oven and cool to room temperature. Turn out onto a parchment-covered cutting board. With a round cookie cutter, cut cake rounds the same diameter as the top of the cups or molds you've selected for the Chocolate-Raspberry Mousse. Set cake rounds aside (may be frozen if necessary).

For Chocolate-Raspberry Mousse: If using frozen raspberries thaw before proceeding.

In the top of a double boiler, melt the milk chocolate over hot water.

In a small saucepan, heat 3/4 cup whipping cream until tiny bubbles form around the edges of the pan. Stir scalded cream into the melted chocolate.

Puree the raspberries and strain out the seeds. You should have 1/2 cup puree (if you have a little bit less make up the rest with water). Stir the seedless puree into the warm chocolate mixture. Set aside to cool to room temperature.

Combine the remaining 1 cup whipping cream with the crème fraiche. Whip to soft peaks and then fold into the cooled chocolate-raspberry mixture. (Note that room temperature is about 70 degrees. If you use your finger to test the chocolate, it should feel cool to the touch; if it feels warm or even tepid, cool the chocolate further. If you fold the whipped cream into warm chocolate the mixture may "break," resulting in a grainy rather than smooth texture).

Fill the ramekins or molds with mousse. Top with the precut cake rounds.

Freeze bombes until firm, at least 3 to 4 hours or overnight. The bombes will not be served frozen, but they are easier to unmold and glaze while frozen.

> Chocolate contains only 1/5 to 1/25th as much caffeine as coffee.

For Chocolate Glaze: Melt the bittersweet chocolate and butter together in the top of a double boiler. Stir frequently to blend well. Keep warm until needed.

To Assemble: Unmold bombes by dipping molds into cool water for 10 to 15 seconds. (Do not use warm water, as this may slightly melt the mousse). Keep the bombes frozen until ready to glaze.

Place the frozen bombes, one or two at a time, on a wire cooling rack on top of a cookie sheet. Rapidly spoon the warm glaze over each of the bombes. Jiggle the cooling rack gently so excess glaze will run off of the bombes. After glazing all the bombes, transfer them to another cookie sheet using a metal spatula. Continue glazing the bombes in this fashion until all are glazed. Glaze only one or two at a time, as the glaze will set fairly quickly. Trying to glaze more than one at a time can result in drips of glaze hardening on the sides of the bombes. Excess glaze can be reserved and used at a later date.

To decorate the glazed bombes, drizzle or stripe with melted white or milk chocolate.

Chef's note: Crème Fraiche is like a mild version of sour cream. If you're pressed for time, you can substitute an equal amount of sour cream for crème fraiche in the mousses. However, the mousses will have a slightly sharper flavor to them.

You can also use this recipe to make one large bombe. Cut cake into pieces to line a one quart freezer proof bowl. Reserve a large enough piece of the cake to use as the bottom of the bombe. Proceed as directed, making sure to allow a longer time for both freezing and thawing.

Spanish Princess Maria Theresa became engaged to Louis XIV of France in 1615. Her gift to Louis was an ornate chest filled with chocolate.

Mousse in a Bag

Mousse in a Bag, the signature chocolate dessert at Whale's Tale in Newport, Oregon, is a delicious and impressive looking dessert that combines white chocolate mousse, dark chocolate "sacks," and fresh berries. Plan to make this dessert a day or two in advance of serving it.

Makes 6 servings

White Chocolate Mousse:
12 1/2 ounces chopped white chocolate
2 1/2 cups whipping cream, divided
5 tablespoons unsalted butter
3 eggs, separated
3 tablespoons orange liqueur, divided
3 teaspoons cherry liqueur, divided
2 teaspoons vanilla, divided
2 tablespoons granulated sugar
3 tablespoons powdered sugar

Chocolate Bags:
1 pound chopped bittersweet chocolate
6 1/2-pound coffee bags, coated on the inside with plastic
2-inch natural bristle paint brush
Pan large enough to hold the 6 coffee bags when open

Presentation:
3 cups fresh berries (use strawberries, raspberries, or blueberries,
    or a combination of the three)
2 tablespoons orange liqueur (optional)
1/2 cup plus 3 tablespoons granulated sugar, divided
1 1/2 cups whipping cream

For White Chocolate Mousse: In the top of a double boiler, melt the white chocolate over hot, not boiling, water. Stir until smooth and keep warm over very low heat.

Place 1 cup whipping cream plus the butter in a heavy saucepan. Chill the remaining cream. Separate the eggs, placing the whites in a mixer bowl and the yolks in a small bowl.

Heat the cream and butter to a gentle boil. Remove from heat and stir a small amount of the cream mixture into the egg yolks. Return this mixture to the saucepan, stirring vigorously. Cook over low heat, while stirring constantly, until the mixture coats the back of a spoon.

Pour this custard into a medium bowl. Stir in 2 tablespoons orange liqueur, 2 teaspoons cherry liqueur, and 1 teaspoon vanilla. Pour in the melted white chocolate while whisking. The mixture will turn a deep golden color.

Whip the egg whites until soft peaks form. Add the granulated sugar and continue beating until the whites are stiff but not dry. Whisk 3/4 of the whites into the chocolate mixture. Fold in the remaining whites using a rubber spatula. Chill for at least 1 hour.

Beat the 1 1/2 cups cream with the remaining 1 tablespoon orange liqueur, 1 teaspoon cherry liqueur, and 1 teaspoon vanilla. When the cream begins to thicken, add the 3 table-spoons powdered sugar. Whip only until soft peaks form, do not over beat. Fold the whipped cream into the custard mixture very thoroughly. Cover with plastic wrap and refrigerate overnight.

For Chocolate Bags: In the top of a double boiler, melt the chocolate over hot, not boiling, water. Keep warm over very low heat.

Cut the tops of the bags off so they are about 2 inches high. Open the bags and keep the sides as straight as possible. Ladle about 2 tablespoons of chocolate into a bag. Dip the brush into the melted chocolate in the pot and use it to paint the inside sides and bottom of the bag. Place the chocolate-coated bag in the pan. Repeat the ladling and painting for each bag. Set the pan of bags into the freezer for about 10 minutes or until the chocolate is set.

> "We used chocolate in the morning…(it) is mild in its effect and at the same time nourishing."
> – Dr. Fridtjob Nasen (1860-1930), one of the first Arctic explorers to cross Greenland.

Remove from freezer and give each bag a second coat of chocolate. Return to the freezer. When the second coat is set, remove the pan from the freezer. Pipe or spoon the white chocolate mousse into each bag. Cover with plastic wrap and freeze 8 hours or over-night. Any leftover bittersweet chocolate can be stored in a clean container and reheated for another use.

For Presentation: Stir together the berries, liqueur, and 1/2 cup sugar, and set aside.

Remove the chocolate bags from the freezer and carefully peel the paper bags from the outside. Place the bags back in the pan or on a tray and refrigerate until serving time.

Just before serving, whip the cream with 3 tablespoons sugar until stiff peaks form. Place about 1/2 cup fruit on each of six plates. Place a mousse bag on each plate and spoon or pipe the whipped cream on top of the bag. Serve.

Recipe Tester's note: The optional orange liqueur in fresh fruit may be too strong for some. This tester prefers the fresh fruit without the added liqueur.

Whale's Tale, Newport, Oregon

Seashell Cakes
with Chocolate Truffle Filling

These delicate chocolate shell cakes are filled with feathery truffle filling.

Makes 20 cupcake sized cakes

Cakes:

4 ounces chopped unsweetened chocolate

6 ounces chopped bittersweet chocolate

11 tablespoons plus 1 teaspoon unsalted butter

1 1/2 cups brewed hot coffee

2 eggs, beaten

1 teaspoon vanilla

2 cups cake flour, sifted

1 cup plus 2 tablespoons granulated sugar

1 teaspoon baking soda

1/4 teaspoon salt

1/4 cup rum

Truffle Centers:

10 ounces chopped bittersweet chocolate

1 cup whipping cream

4 tablespoons butter, room temperature

3 tablespoons granulated sugar

3 tablespoons rum

Glaze:

16 ounces chopped bittersweet chocolate

1/3 cup vegetable oil

For Cakes: Preheat oven to 350 degrees. Spray a cast-iron seashell mold pan or a muffin pan with non-stick spray.

In a heavy 2-quart saucepan, combine the chocolates, butter and coffee. Cook and stir over low heat until the chocolates are melted and the mixture is smooth. Remove from heat and let cool for 10 minutes.

While the chocolate is cooling, beat the eggs and vanilla lightly in a small bowl. Set aside.

In another small bowl, stir together the flour, sugar, baking soda, and salt.

Add the rum and the egg mixture to the cooled chocolate mixture. Whisk the flour mixture into the chocolate mixture until smooth.

Spoon the batter into the prepared pan, filling two-thirds full. Bake for 20 to 30 minutes. Baking time will depend on the size of the pans. A toothpick inserted in the center of a cake should come out clean. Cool on wire rack for 20 minutes before removing from pans. Finish cooling on racks.

For Truffle Centers: In the top of a double boiler, melt the chocolate over hot, not boiling, water. Do not let any water touch the chocolate. Keep warm.

Mix the cream, butter, and sugar in a large heavy saucepan. Cook and stir over medium heat until the sugar is dissolved. Bring to a boil. Remove from heat. Carefully stir the melted chocolate into the hot cream mixture. Add rum. Cool.

For Glaze: In the top of a double boiler, melt the chocolate and oil over hot, not boiling, water. Stir until smooth. Keep warm until ready to use.

Assembly: Turn the cakes upside down. With a melon baller or other small sharp spoon, remove a chunk from the middle of each cake. The size of the chunk will vary with the size of the cakes. Fill the hole with some of the truffle filling.

Turn cakes right side up and place on a rack over a large rimmed cookie sheet. Ladle the glaze over each cake slowly to cover and make a smooth surface. Let cakes stand undisturbed on the rack until the glaze is set. Remove to a serving plate with a spatula.

Chef's note: If you have an truffle filling left over, roll into balls and dust with cocoa for a delightful treat. Any left over glaze may be refrigerated for several weeks and reheated for another use like ice cream topping.

Recipe Tester's note: Truffle filling may be easily piped into cakes using a pastry bag.

"Don't wreck a sublime chocolate experience by feeling guilty. Chocolate isn't like premarital sex. It will not make you pregnant. And it always feels good."

— Lora Brady,
Growing Up on the
Chocolate Diet

Glossary

Chefs, bakers, and chocolatiers use terms, many of them foreign, that you may or may not be familiar with (approximate pronunciation in italic).

Amaretto *(am-ah-reht-toh)* - An almond-flavored liqueur.

Bain marie *(bahn mah-ree)* - French for water bath.

Blanch - To plunge food into boiling water briefly, then into cold water to stop the cooking process.

Blend - To mix two or more ingredients together with a spoon, beater, or mixer to combine.

Bloom - Pale grey streaks and blotches that appear on the surface of chocolate that has gotten too hot. It's caused by cocoa butter crystals migrating to the surface.

Bombe - *(bomb)* - A cylindrical or bomb-shaped dessert consisting of mousse or ice cream with mousse.

Bundt pan *(buhnt)* - A tube cake pan with fluted sides.

Caramelize *(kar-ah-meh-lyz)* - To heat sugar until it melts into a clear syrup and turns golden to deep brown (320 to 350 degrees).

Chocolate buttercream - A very light frosting made from chocolate, egg whites, sugar, and butter.

Coulis *(cou-lee)* - Thin purée or sieved sauce made of fruit or vegetables.

Couverture *(co-va-tur)* - Chocolate for dipping or coating renown for its shiny, smooth quality ("couverture" is French for "covering"). This highly-refined chocolate has a higher cocoa butter content (about half its weight) than eating or baking chocolate and forms a thin, hard, shiny shell.

Cream - *n.* When unhomogenized milk is left to sit, it separates into thick, milk-fat rich cream on top and lower-fat milk on the bottom. *v.* To beat one or more ingredients until smooth, soft, and creamy.

Crème anglaise *(crem anglaze)* - A light vanilla sauce or thick custard made from milk, vanilla bean, egg yolks, and sugar.

Crème brulee *(crem bru-lay)* - Baked custard cream with a burnt sugar topping.

Crème chantilly or chantilly cream - Whipped cream flavored with vanilla.

Crème fraiche *(crem frash)* - A mature and tangy cream that's made from heavy cream and buttermilk or sour cream that has soured and thickened to the consistency of yogurt.

Curacao *(kyoor-uh-soh)* - An orange-flavored liqueur.

Custard - A pudding-like dessert made with milk, eggs, sugar, and flavorings that is baked in a water bath or cooked on the stovetop.

Ganache (ga-naash)- A smooth cream made from mixing chocolate and boiled cream.

Gelatin *(jehl-uh-tihn)* - An odorless, tasteless, colorless thickener that is dissolved in warm water. When cooled, it forms a jelly.

Genoise *(zhehn-wah)* - A rich, light cake made from flour, sugar, eggs, vanilla, and butter that's similar in texture to moist sponge cake.

Grappa - Originally, a traditional "winter warmer" produced in the mountains of Italy, grappa is a clear spirit made from bits of the grape after the juice has been pressed out.

Hazelnut flour - Flour made from mixing finely-ground hazelnuts and all-purpose flour in a 2 to 1 ratio of nuts to flour. Pastry chef Diana Vineyard Copeland calls hazelnut flour her "secret ingredient."

Jelly-roll pan - A rectangular pan with 1-inch deep sides used to make sheet cakes or sponge cakes for jelly rolls.

Knead *(need)* - A process of mixing and working dough into a cohesive, pliable mass. It may be accomplished by using a mixer with a dough hook, a food processor with a plastic blade, or by hand by folding the dough in half, turning one-quarter, folding in half, etc.

Ladyfinger - Light, delicate sponge cake that is shaped into long, fat "fingers." Used to make desserts like tiramisu and charlottes.

Madeleines *(mad-e-lynns)* - Shell-shaped sponge cakes.

Marjolaine *(mar-jo-lane)* - A dessert made of sponge cake, custard cream, buttercream, and cake crumbs.

Mascarpone cheese *(mas-kar-Pohn)* - A rich Italian double or triple cream cheese. It's used in tiramisu and other desserts.

Meringue *(mer-ang)* - A frothy mixture of egg white and sugar that's oven-dried (not baked).

Mousse *(moose)* - A light dessert consisting of whipped cream, egg yolks, boiled sugar, and flavoring.

> Even though the cocoa butter in chocolate is saturated fat, studies have shown that it doesn't raise LDL "bad" blood cholesterol.

Mousseline *(moose-a-leen)* - An egg-sugar base to which lightly whipped cream is added.

Nougat - A confection made with sugar or honey, roasted nuts, and sometimes candied fruit. May be made with egg white (white nougat) or caramelized sugar (brown nougat).

Pastry bag - Cone shaped bag with two open ends. The small, pointed end may be fitted with decorative tips. Fillings are spooned into the larger end. When the bag is squeezed, the fillings are forced out of tip.

Pastry brush - A small brush used for applying glazes to baked goods.

Pot de crème *(po-da-crem)* - Custard baked and served in a cup.

Pound cake - Fine-textured cake made of flour, butter, vanilla, and eggs. The name comes from the fact that this cake was originally made with a pound each of the ingredients. It's usually flavored with lemon or vanilla.

Praline *(pray-leen)* - Paste made from sugar, almonds, and other nuts. May also refer to nuts carmelized with sugar.

Puff pastry - A rich, delicate pastry consisting of many layers.

Ramekin *(ram-ih-kihn)* - An individual baking dish (usually 3-4 inches in diameter).

Roulade *(ru-lad)* - Rolled cake.

Scald - To heat a liquid to just below boiling. Tiny bubbles will form on the sides of the pan.

Seize *(seez)* - Melted chocolate that suddenly becomes a thick, lumpy mass. It's caused when a small amount of liquid or steam comes in contact with the chocolate. May be corrected by adding butter, cocoa butter, or vegetable oil.

Sorbet *(sor-bay)* - A well-flavored, semi-frozen ice.

Soufflé *(soo-flay)* - A very light, baked, or steamed pudding or dessert.

Sponge cake - A light yet rich cake that gets its lightness from beaten egg whites.

Springform pan - A round pan with high, straight sides that expands with the aid of a spring or clamp. The bottom of the pan is removable. Springform pans are often used to make cheesecakes.

Tiramisu *(tih-ruh-mee-soo)* - A classic Italian dessert made with sponge cake or lady-fingers dipped in espresso and marsala, rum, or Kahlua, mascarpone cheese (ultra-rich cream cheese), grated chocolate, and, sometimes, whipped cream.

Water bath - Also called a bain marie, this cooking technique calls for placing a container into a large, shallow pan of water, which surrounds the food with gentle heat. A water bath may be used in the oven or on the top of the stove.

Whip - *v.* To beat ingredients and introduce air until they are light and fluffy.

White chocolate - A mixture of cocoa butter, sugar, milk solids, lecithin, and vanilla. Because it doesn't contain chocolate liquor, white chocolate isn't classified as real chocolate.

Appendix I

Resources

Catalogues for Chocolate and Baking-Related Items

Sweet Celebrations (formerly Maid of Scandinavia)
7009 Washington Avenue South
Edina, MN 55439
(800) 328-6722
> *In addition to baking and candy making supplies, they sell Callebaut, Valhrona, Peter's, Lindt, and Merckens chocolate.*

King Arthur Flour Baker's Catalog
P.O. Box 876
Norwich, VT 05055
(800) 827-6836
> *In addition to baking supplies, they sell Guittard chocolate.*

Sur La Table
Catalog Division
1765 Sixth Avenue South
Seattle, WA 98134
(800) 243-0852
http://www.surlatable.com
> *They sell a large array of kitchen items, including many hard-to-find baking tools.*
>
> *Sur La Table also has several wonderful retail stores stocked with just about every baking and cooking tool imaginable. Exploring them is a great way to spend an afternoon.*

Washington	*California*	
Pike Place Market	1806 Fourth St.	161 W Colorado Blvd.
84 Pine St.	Berkeley, CA	Pasadena, CA
Seattle, WA	(510) 849-2252	(626) 744- 9987
(206) 448-2244		
	832 Avocado Ave.	77 Maiden Ln.
90 Central Way	Newport Beach, CA	San Francisco, CA
Kirkland, WA	(949) 640-0200	(415) 732-7900
(425) 827-1311		

301 Wilshire Blvd.
Santa Monica, CA
(310) 395-0390

23 University Ave.
Los Gatos, CA
(408) 395-6946

4050 E. Thousand
   Oaks Blvd.
Thousand Oaks, CA
(805) 381-0030

Colorado
Eleven Cherry Creek
300 E. 1st Ave.
Denver, CO
(303) 780-7900

Texas
4527 Travis St., Suite A
Dallas, TX
(214) 219-4404

Chocolate Sources

You can usually find good chocolate at upscale, specialty food markets or baking supply companies. Many retail chocolate shops like Fran's Chocolates in Seattle, Washington, and Bernard C. in Oregon and Washington, or Bernard Callebaut in Canada are now carrying good-quality chocolate for bakers. You can also contact the chocolate manufacturers directly to find stores in your area that carry their chocolates. However, the best place to buy chocolate in bulk may be from a local candy wholesaler – check the yellow pages.

If you do a good amount of chocolate baking and dessert making, we suggest you buy at least 10-pound blocks of good-quality chocolate (imported varieties come in 11-pound blocks). It's usually less expensive than buying smaller bars or by weight in chunks and you'll be surprised at how quickly you'll use it. Some chocolate companies will not ship during the summer months and those who ship via United Parcel Service (UPS) won't ship to post office boxes.

Ghirardelli Chocolate Company
111 139th Ave.
San Leandro, CA 94578
(800) 488-0078

Merckens Chocolate
150 Oakland St.
Mansfield, MA 02048
(800) 637-2536

Scharffen Berger Chocolate Maker
250 South Maple Ave.
South San Francisco, CA 94080
(800) 930-4528

Paradigm Food Works
5775 SW Jean Rd., suite 106A
Lake Oswego, OR 97035
(800) 234-0250/(503) 636-4880
> *They sell Ghirardelli, Guittard, Lindt, Merckens, and Peter's chocolate.*

Sweet Celebrations (see listing under catalogues)

Gourmail
126A Pleasant Valley St. #401
Methuen, MA 01844
(800) 366-5900
http://www.gourmail.com
> *They sell Cacoa Barry, Callebaut, and Peter's Chocolate, and Valhrona.*

On-line Resources

There are plenty of on-line markets opening every day. Many sell up-scale bakeware and kitchen items. Some offer chocolate from around the world. If you've got access to the Web, try these sites.

Digital Chef
http://www.digitalchef.com
> *They offer bakeware and other kitchen items.*

The Chef's Store (888) 334-CHEF
http://www.chefsstore.com
> *This site offers baking items.*

Chocolate Epicure
http://www.chocolateepicure.com
> *They sell a variety of high-quality chocolate, including Lindt, Valhrona, Callebaut, Scharffen Berger, and El Rey.*

Gourmet Market
http://www.gourmetmarket.com
> *They sell cookware and chocolate, including Callebaut, El Rey, Lindt, Scarffen Berger, Michael Cluizel, and others.*

Hershey Corporation
http://www.hersheys.com
> *The folks at Hershey offer chocolate recipes as well as a consumer line you can call with questions about the recipes and/or their chocolate.*

Publications

Chocolatier Magazine
45 West 34th Street, suite 600
New York, NY 10001
(212) 239-0855
The magazine for chocolate lovers.

Sources/Recommended Reading

The Chocolate Bible, Christian Teubner, Penguin Books, New York, NY, 1997. The sourcebook for chocophiles. Incredible photos and highly readable text on all aspects of chocolate.

Growing Up on the Chocolate Diet, Lora Brody, Little and Brown, New York, NY 1985. A funny, irreverent memoir with recipes by a dedicated chocophile.

Chocolate Fads, Folklore, and Fantasies, Linda K. Fuller, Ph.D., Harrington Park Press, The Haworth Press, Inc. Binghamton, NY, 1994. A wonderfully entertaining book of trivia about chocolate.

Hershey's Chocolate and Cocoa Cookbook, Ideal Publishing Corporation, Milwaukie, WI. This classic has a wonderful section on chocolate and cocoa basics.

Mrs. Fields I Love Chocolate Cookbook, Time Life Books, New York, NY 1994. If you like beautiful chocolate photos and easy-to-make desserts, you'll like this cookbook.

Truffles and Other Chocolate Confections, Holt, Rinehart, and Winston, New York NY 1984. This is a classic primer for chocolate cooks who want to make great truffles.

Sweet Seduction, Chocolate Truffles, Adrienne Welch, Harper and Row, New York, NY 1984. Another wonderful book on making truffles, the Mercedes of chocolate candy.

The Kids' Book of Chocolate, Richard Ammon, Atheneum, NY, 1987. This is a great book for children that gives plenty of interesting information about chocolate.

Metric Conversions

Teaspoon Equivalents

U.S. MEASURE		METRIC MEASURE
1/8 teaspoon	=	0.5 ml. (milliliters)
1/4 teaspoon	=	1.5ml.
1/2 teaspoon	=	3 ml.
3/4 teaspoon	=	4 ml.
1 teaspoon	=	5 ml. or 5.0 g. (grams)
1 tablespoon(3 teaspoons or 1/2 ounce)	=	15 ml. or 14.3 g.
2 tablespoons (1 ounce)	=	30 ml. or 28.35 g.
3 tablespoons	=	45 ml.

Cup Equivalents

1/4 cup (4 tablespoons or 2 ounces)	=	60 ml.
1/3 cup	=	85 ml.
1/2 cup (8 tablespoons or 4 ounces)	=	125 ml.
2/3 cup	=	170 ml.
3/4 cup	=	180 ml.
1 cup (8 ounces or 1/2 pound)	=	250 ml.
1 1/4 cup	=	310 ml.
1 1/2 cup	=	375 ml.
2 cups (32 tablespoons, 16 ounces or 1 pound)	=	500 ml.
3 cups	=	750 ml.
4 cups (1 quart, 32 ounces, or 2 pounds)	=	Approx. 1 liter

Pan Sizes

1 inch	=	2.5 cm (centimeters)
8-inch square	=	30-cm. square
13 x 9 x 1 1/2-inch	=	33 x 23 x 4 cm.
13 x 9 x 2-inch	=	33 x 23 x 5 cm.
12 x 7 1/2 x 1 1/2-inch	=	30 x 18 x 4
10 x 6 x 2-inch	=	25 x 15 x 5 cm.
9 x 5 x 3-inch (loaf pan)	=	23 x 13 x 8 cm.
1 quart baking dish	=	1 liter
2 quart baking dish	=	2 liter
5-6 cup ring mold	=	1.5 liters

Oven Temperatures: Fahrenheit (F.) to Celsius (C)

275 degrees F.		=	135 degrees C.
300 degrees F.		=	149 degrees C.
325 degrees F.		=	165 degrees C.
350 degrees F.	(baking)	=	175 degrees C.
375 degrees F.		=	190 degrees C.
400 degrees F.	(hot oven)	=	205 degrees C.
425 degrees F.		=	218 degrees C.
450 degrees F.	(very hot oven)	=	230 degrees C.
500 degrees F.	(broiling)	=	260 degrees C.

To convert from Fahrenheit to Celsius: Subtract 32 from Fahrenheit figure, multiply by 5, then divide by 9 to get Celsius.

Conversion Factors

RECIPE CALLS FOR	MULTIPLY BY	FOR
teaspoons (tsp)	5	milliliters (ml.)
tablespoons (tbsp.	15	milliliters (ml.)
fluid ounces (fl. oz.)	30	milliliters (ml.)
cups (c.)	0.24	liters (l.)
pints (pt.)	0.47	liters (l.)
quarts (qt.)	0.95	liters (l.)
ounces (oz.)	28.3	grams (g.)
pounds (lb.)	0.45	kilograms (kg.)

Appendix III
Featured Restaurants, Bakeries, & Inns

Anjou Bakery and Catering
3898 Old Monitor Highway
Cashmere, WA
(509) 782-4360

Apple Cellar Bakery and Rotisserie
2255 Highway 66
Ashland, OR
(541) 488-8131

ARR Place
143 SW Cliff Street
Newport, OR
(541) 265-4240

Bacchus Restaurant
(Wedgewood Hotel)
845 Hornby
Vancouver, B.C., Canada
(604) 689-7777

Bella Union
170 W California
Jacksonville, OR
(541) 899-1770

The Belmont
925 Water Street
Port Townsend, WA
(360) 385-3007

Berlin Inn
3131 SE 12th
Portland, OR
(503) 236-6761

Birchfield Manor Country Inn
2018 Birchfield Road
Yakima, WA
(509) 452-1960/800-375-3420

Black Butte Ranch Dining Room
Black Butte Ranch, OR
(541) 595-1260

Bread and Roses Bakery
230 Quincy Street
Port Townsend, WA
(360) 385-1044

The Brewery
509 SW G Street
Grants Pass, OR
(541) 479-9850

Broken Top Restaurant
62000 Broken Top Drive
Bend, OR
(541) 383-8210

Bugatti's Ristorante Italiano
18740 Willamette Drive
West Linn, OR
(503) 636-9555

Café de Amis
1987 NW Kearny
Portland, OR
(503) 295-6487

Campagne
86 Pine Street
Seattle, WA
(206) 728-2800

Canlis Restaurant
2576 Aurora Avenue N
Seattle, WA
(206) 283-3313

Caprial's Bistro and Wine
7015 SE Milwaukie Avenue
Portland, OR
(503) 236-6457

Cheri Walker's 42nd Street Café
4201 Pacific Way
Seaview, WA
(360) 642-2323

Chez Shea
94 Pike Street, suite 34
Seattle, WA
(206) 467-9990

Coho Grill and Catering
(Orion Greens Golf Course)
61535 Fargo Lane
Bend, OR
(541) 388-3909

Decadence Café and Catering
1724 Douglas Street
Victoria, B.C., Canada
(250) 389-0383

Deli de Pasta
7 North Front Street
Yakima, WA
(509) 453-0571

Diva at the Met
(Metropolitan Hotel)
645 Howe Street
Vancouver, B.C., Canada
(604) 602-7788

Duck Soup Inn
3090 Roche Harbor Road
Friday Harbor, WA
(360) 378-4878

Fleuri Restaurant
(The Sutton Place Hotel)
845 Burrard Street
Vancouver, B.C., Canada
(604) 682-5511

Flying Fish
2234 First Avenue
Seattle, WA
(206) 728-8595

Fountain Café
920 Washington Street
Port Townsend, WA
(360) 385-1364

Fran's Chocolate
2594 NE University Village
Seattle, WA
(206) 528-9969

Other NW location:
10305 NE 10th Street
Bellevue, WA
(425) 453-1698

Gasperetti's
1013 N 1st Street
Yakima, WA
(509) 248-0628

Geiser Grand Hotel
1996 Main Street
Baker City, OR
(541) 523-1889

Genoa
2832 SE Belmont
Portland, OR
(503) 238-1464

Georgia's Bakery
109 N 1st Street, suite 105
La Conner, WA
(360) 466-2149

Gerry Frank's Konditorei
310 Kearny Street SE
Salem, OR
(503) 585-7070

The Grateful Bread Bakery
34805 Brooten Road
Pacific City, OR
(503) 965-7337

Home Fires Bakery
13013 Bayne Road
Leavenworth, WA
(509) 548-7362

The Hunt Club
(Sorrento Hotel)
900 Madison
Seattle, WA
(206) 343-6156

Il Giardino di Umberto
1382 Hornby Street
Vancouver, B.C., Canada
(604) 669-2422

Il Terrazzo Carmine
411 1st Avenue S
Seattle, WA
(206) 467-7797

**John Horan's
Steak and Seafood House**
2 Horan Road
Wenatchee, WA
(509) 663-0018

Just American Desserts
10625 E Sprague
Spokane, WA
(509) 927-2253

Other Spokane locations:
2812 E 30th Avenue
(509) 534-7195

6406 N Monroe Street
(509) 328-5889

Kaspar's
19 W Harrison Street
Seattle, WA
(206) 298-0123

L'Auberge
2601 NW Vaughn Street
Portland, OR
(503) 223-3302

**La Conner Seafood
and Prime Rib House**
614 1st Street
La Conner, WA
(360) 466-4014

La Petite Restaurant
3401 Commercial Avenue
Anacortes, WA
(360) 293-4644

Le Crocodile
909 Burrard, suite 100
Vancouver, B.C., Canada
(604) 669-4298

London Grill
(Benson Hotel)
309 SW Broadway
Portland, OR
(503) 295-4110

Lord Bennett's
Restaurant and Lounge
1695 Beach Loop Drive
Bandon, OR
(541) 347-3663

Luna
5620 S Perry Street
Spokane, WA
(509) 448-2383

Oyster Creek Inn
2190 Chuckanut Drive
Bow, WA
(360) 766-6816

Pacific Café
100 N Commercial Street
Bellingham, WA
(360) 647-0800

Paley's Place
1204 NW 21st Avenue
Portland, OR
(503) 243-2403

Papa Haydn
5829 SE Milwaukie Avenue
Portland, OR
(503) 232-9440

Other Portland location:
701 NW 23rd Avenue
(503) 228-7317

Pastazza
Barkley Village
2945 Newmarket Street, suite 101
Bellingham, WA
(360) 714-1168

Pazzo Ristorante
(Hotel Vintage Plaza)
627 SW Washington
Portland, OR
(503) 228-1515

Prospector Pies
731 N Wenatchee Avenue
Wenatchee, WA
(509) 662-1118

The Place Next to
the San Juan Ferry
1 Spring Street
Friday Harbor, WA
(360) 378-8707

Red Star Tavern
and Roast House
503 SW Alder
Portland, OR
(503) 222-0005

Restaurant at Awbrey Glen
(Awbrey Glen Golf Course)
2500 NW Awbrey Glen Drive
Bend, OR
(541) 317-2885

Rhodendron Café
5521 Chuckanut Drive
Bow, WA
(360) 766-6667

RiverPlace Hotel
1510 SW Harbor Way
Portland, OR
(503) 295-6166

Serafina
2043 Eastlake Avenue E
Seattle, WA
(206) 323-0807

Ship Bay Oyster House
326 Olga Road (Horseshoe Highway)
Eastsound, WA
(360) 376-5886

Silverwater Café
237 Taylor Street
Port Townsend, WA
(360) 385-6448

Skamania Lodge
1131 Skamania Lodge Way
Stevenson, WA.
(509) 427-7700/
(888) SKAMANIA

Suzanne's Specialty Baking
1305 Meador Avenue, suite B#1
Bellingham, WA
(360) 676-0747

Tables of Content
(Sylvia Beach Hotel)
267 NW Cliff Street
Newport, OR
(541) 265-5428

**Teahouse Restaurant
at Ferguson Point**
7501 Stanley Park Drive
Vancouver, B.C., Canada
(604) 669-3281

Tidal Raves
279 NW Highway 101
Depoe Bay, OR
(541) 765-2995

Villa del Lupo
869 Hamilton Street
Vancouver, B.C., Canada
(604) 688-7436

Visconti's
1737 N Wenatchee Avenue
Wenatchee, WA
(509) 662-5013

The Wayfarer
(Surf Sand Resort)
1190 Pacific Drive
Cannon Beach, OR
(503) 436-1108

Whale's Tale
452 SW Bay Boulevard
Newport, OR
(541) 265-8660

The White Swan Guest House
15872 Moore Road
Mt. Vernon, WA
(360) 445-6805

Wild Garlic
114 Prospect Street
Bellingham, WA
(360) 671-1955

Wildflowers Restaurant
2001 E College Way
Mt. Vernon, WA
(360) 424-9724

The William Tell Restaurant
(Georgian Court Hotel)
765 Beatty Street
Vancouver, B.C., Canada
(604) 688-3504

Windows of the Seasons
(Cavanaugh's Inn at the Park)
W 303 North River Drive
Spokane, WA
(509) 328-9526

Zefiro
500 NW 21st Avenue
Portland, OR
(503) 226-3394

3 Doors Down
1429 SE 37th Avenue
Portland, OR
(503) 236-6886

Index

If you love chocolate and you love traveling in Oregon, Washington, and British Columbia, you'll love *The Chocolate Lover's Guide to the Pacific Northwest.* It's the newest and most delicious guidebook to everything chocolate in the Pacific Northwest.

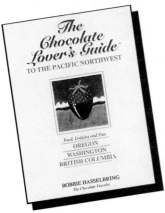

✔ Divided by region.
✔ Easy to use.
✔ 320 pages.
✔ Indexed.
✔ Lists terrific hotels and bed and breakfasts.
✔ Fun things to do.
✔ Chocolate Best List.
✔ Reviews 400+ restaurants, bakeries, ice creameries, and chocolate shops that make terrific chocolate.

"The Chocolate Lover's Guide is crammed with information the traveler and the chocolate lover needs. The author's deft, lighthearted touch makes you want to keep on reading. Like a box of perfect chocolates, it's delicious and you can't stop with just a taste." – **Marilyn McFarlane**, author *Best Places to Stay in the Pacific Northwest, Best Places to Stay in California*

"I love The Chocolate Lover's Guide! As a chocolate devotee, I find this book to be invaluable in seeking the finer things in life." – **Kay Allenbaugh**, author *Chocolate for a Woman's Soul*

"...a mouthwatering, mind-boggling compendium of just about every chocolate treat worth eating from John Day to Vancouver, British Columbia." – **Heidi Yorkshire**, *The Oregonian* newspaper

Only $17.95, plus shipping. **Order 2 copies and get 10% off.**
Use the order form following.

Attention Fund Raisers!

Everyone loves chocolate! In fact, chocolate is the #1 flavor in North America. We spend $7 billion annually on chocolate. You can put chocolate to work for you and your organization by using *The Chocolate Lover's Guide* and *The Chocolate Lover's Cookbook* as a fundraiser. Generous quantity discounts are available. Call toll-free 1-877-800-7700 for more information.

Order Form

The Chocolate Lover's Guide Cookbook and *The Chocolate Lover's Guide to the Pacific Northwest*, a complete travel guide, make wonderful gifts for yourself, or for chocolate-loving friends, family, and co-workers. Order 2 of either book or one of each and get 10% off.

Send me:

___ *The Chocolate Lover's Guide Cookbook* @ $18.95 each $ _____

___ *The Chocolate Lover's Guide to the Pacific Northwest* @ $17.95 each $ _____

Shipping and handling for up to 2 books $4.00 $ _____

     Each additional book $1.50 $ _____

10% discount for ordering 2 books $ _____

Total order amount $ _____

Name_____

Address _____

City, State, or Province, Zip/Postal Code _____

Country _____ Daytime phone number _____

I'd like my copy autographed _____

Any special message _____

Mail this order with your check or money order to:
     Wordsworth Publishing
     P.O. Box 311
     Beavercreek, OR 97004

Phone or Fax Orders:
     Call (503) 632-4610 (Portland, OR area)
     or toll-free 1-877-800-7700 (outside Portland area only)
     or fax (503) 632-6754.

Credit Card No. _____

____ Visa _____ MC (check one)   Expiration date _____

WORDWORTH PUBLISHING'S 100%, NO HASSLE, MONEY-BACK GUARANTEE

We're so confident that you'll love the books we publish, we offer a 100% money-back guarantee. If, for any reason, you're not completely satisfied with one of our books, send it back with your receipt and a note telling us the problem and we'll refund your money promptly. We guarantee it!